PRAISE FOR BARBARA PIERCE
AND HER NOVELS

Naughty by Nature

"I____ a delightful and poignant romance that touch-
e____ ions. . . . [H]er wonderfully drawn characters
a____ ing and her story compelling."
—*Romantic Times BOOKreviews*

"P____ rce always delivers to her readers a story filled
w____ n, romance, and just a touch of whimsy that
k____ eaders coming back for more time and time
a____
—*A Romance Review*

"Ms. Pierce has once again enthralled me with her captivating storytelling abilities…I was immersed from the
first page to the last and encourage new readers to experience the thrill from this captivating new author. Highly
recommended!" —*Kwips and Kritiques*

Sinful Between the Sheets

"The second title in her enticing series pairs extraordinary
characters in a sexually charged situation that allows you
to explore a few fantasies of your own."
—*Romantic Times BOOKreviews*

"Pierce weaves ____ igue and
steamy love s____ d twists,
witty dialogu____

____s Weekly

MORE . . .

"Pierce reaches new heights in this titillating, spicy romance as she plays upon our wicked fantasies while crafting a fine-tuned tale of revenge and sizzling desire."
—*Romantic Times BOOKreviews*

"Barbara Pierce's star continues to rise!"
—Gaelen Foley, national bestselling author

Courting the Countess

"Pierce carries off just-simmering-underneath sexual tension like a virtuoso and keeps readers wondering just how these two dynamic characters will get together. This splendid read shimmers with the temptation of seduction and the healing power of love."
—*Romantic Times BOOKreviews*

"Pierce once again earns our appreciation for delighting us with her talent."
—*Rendezvous*

"A good storyline...a nice read."
—*The Best Reviews*

"Impossible to put down...[Pierce is] a truly exceptional storyteller."
—*Romance Reader at Heart*

Tempting the Heiress

"Pierce does an excellent job blending danger and intrigue into the plot of her latest love story. Readers who like their Regency historicals a bit darker and spiked with realistic grit will love this wickedly sexy romance."
—*Booklist*

Scandalous
by Night

BARBARA PIERCE

St. Martin's Paperbacks

This is a work of fiction. All of the characters, organizations and events portrayed in this novel are either products of the author's imagination or are used fictitiously.

SCANDALOUS BY NIGHT

Copyright © 2008 by Barbara Pierce.

Cover photograph © Herman Estevez.

For information address St. Martin's Press, 175 Fifth Avenue, New York, NY 10010.

ISBN: 0-312-94797-6
EAN: 978-0-312-94797-2

Printed in the United States of America

St. Martin's Paperbacks edition / August 2008

St. Martin's Paperbacks are published by St. Martin's Press, 175 Fifth Avenue, New York, NY 10010.

10 9 8 7 6 5 4 3 2 1

For my brother, Brian. From childhood playmate to Webmaster extraordinaire— you're the best!

When soul meets soul on lovers' lips.
—Percy Bysshe Shelley, *Prometheus Unbound*

PROLOGUE
November 12, 1799, Worrington Hall

Hate.

The insidious emotion slithered like a parasite just beneath his skin; whispering enticing promises of retribution as it slowly consumed a man's soul. Townsend Elliot Lidsaw, Viscount Everod, had not truly embraced the darker side of his nature until his defiant, fuming gaze had settled on the small, pale, beautiful face of Maura Keighly, knowing the ten-year-old girl had cost him his family.

The girl stood, her slender frame trembling, between Everod's father and his thirteen-year-old younger brother, Rowan. Even in anger, he conceded that she was a beautiful creature with unblemished alabaster skin, a pert nose he had enjoyed tweaking on numerous occasions, and a prodigious wealth of dark brown ringlets that saucily framed her face. At present, her nose and cheeks were an unflattering pink and her sea-gray eyes were red and swollen from crying. Did she weep for him or herself? Everod had pondered the question since her calculated betrayal seven days earlier. Each night, he had heard Maura's muffled sobs long past midnight when both of them should have been sleeping.

Everod deliberately touched his bandaged throat as he strolled through the front marble hall of the country house that had been in his family for three generations. Maura's sweet, duplicitous face blanched to an alarming pallor. Swaying, she touched his brother's arm for support. Her distress warmed him like mulled wine on a winter's evening.

Yes, you lying bitch. I know the sins that slipped effortlessly from your lips.

The wound at his throat had almost been mortal. The blade had caught him just behind his left ear, and cut an ugly jagged path diagonally across his throat to his collarbone. If he had not twisted away during the attack, his father might have succeeded in severing his head from his neck.

Killing his elder son had been the earl's burning intention, after all.

And where was his charming young stepmother, Lady Worrington? The countess had gone to so much trouble to orchestrate his ousting from the family, Everod was surprised that she was not watching the tragic debacle firsthand.

Everod halted parallel to his father, Rowan, and Maura. "Any final words for your heir, Father?" Everod said, his voice so low and hoarse he did not recognize it. "Mayhap a blessing for a speedy and safe journey?"

His father's face flushed bright red at the taunt. His sire might have attacked his heir if not for the two footmen and his younger brother who held the old man's arms.

"You traitorous bastard! I wish you a speedy journey to hell," his father shouted, still seething and struggling to free his arms from his well-meaning captors. "I will rejoice when word reaches me of your death!"

"As will I, Father. As much as you desire to eliminate me as your heir, you cannot prevent me from claiming what is rightfully mine. One day I will claim your title and wealth for my very own as I did your delectable, willing bride just seven days earlier."

"Scoundrel!"

Everod smirked at the insult. If he was indeed a scoundrel, then he intended to revel in his infamy. With a little dedication, he might even become one of the most renowned scoundrels in London!

His hot, insolent amber gaze slid over the cowering girl. Maura could not bear to look at him now that he was close enough to touch her. The temptation to grab her by the throat and choke her until she begged for his mercy made his fingers clench in anticipation.

"Although our parting pains me," he said roughly, his hand absently caressing his bandaged throat, "find solace in the knowledge that we will all meet again." His cold gaze swept over the trio, before finally settling on Maura. Sensing his perusal, she warily lifted her lashes until she saw the heated oath in his amber eyes.

"I know I will."

CHAPTER 1
February 3, 1811, Worrington Hall

"Just as I thought," Georgette Lidsaw, Countess of Worrington, said as she peered at her niece's reflection through the looking glass. "The necklace suits you. Consider it a gift."

Awed by her aunt's generosity, Maura Keighly fingered the silver pendant. It was a beautiful old piece. Composed of two hinged pieces of elaborate silver filigree, the necklace's upper tier had one pearl mounted in the center with two polished silver beads on each side. The bottom portion was in the shape of an upside-down triangle. Three pearls were mounted on each point, the largest at the bottom. Pear-shaped silver beads dangled below the pearls. Shaking her head, Maura reached up to the clasp in an attempt to remove the necklace.

"You spoil me, Georgette, with your generosity. However, I cannot accept your gift." The silver chain slithered through her fingers as she extended her palm to her aunt.

The countess's brow furrowed, reflecting her puzzlement. At six and thirty, Georgette was fourteen years older than her niece. In Maura's opinion, the passing years had only refined the perfection nature had bestowed on her aunt. Georgette had married well, twice. Lord Perton had married her before the end of her aunt's first season in London. The marriage was a happy, albeit brief one. Illness had claimed the lady's beloved lord before her twenty-first birthday.

Maura's mother, Georgette's older sister, had once confessed that her younger sibling had grown reckless in her grief. In a futile attempt to keep pace with the wilder members of the *ton,* Georgette's lavish spending depleted the funds her late husband had set aside for her. By the age of six and twenty, her gambling debts had ruined her. For a lady in her dire financial predicament, her aunt had two choices: she could retire to the country and rely on the charity of her sister, or she could seek out a wealthy husband. The young dowager turned her attentions to the Earl of Worrington. Thirty years her senior, Lord Worrington was immediately smitten. The earl was no stranger to the marriage bed. There had been three other Lady Worringtons before the earl made Georgette his fourth. After twelve years together, both seemed satisfied with the arrangement.

Georgette waved away Maura's extended hand. "Nonsense. The necklace looks lovely on you. Unless you do not like it. Perhaps one of the others . . ." She peered into her case where several other necklaces were coiled like serpents of silver and gold.

"No, Aunt." Maura lightly touched the other woman on the arm. "Georgette, I adore the pendant. Truly." She gazed wistfully at the gleaming silver in her palm. "However, I cannot accept something that is clearly an antique. You can not cast off jewelry that was clearly meant to be worn by the Countess of Worrington."

Georgette tipped her head back and laughed. "Oh, you are a treasure, Maura. This isn't one of the revered Worrington family pieces. The necklace is an old trinket that belonged to a forgotten lady connected to the family. If you do not want it, I suppose we could take it to London with us. We'll visit a silversmith who could melt it down into something more to your liking."

Maura closed her fingers over the pendant. The notion of destroying such a beautiful old piece was abhorrent to her. "That will not be necessary, Aunt. If Lord Worrington does not mind my claiming the necklace, then I will gratefully accept your gift."

She reached up to secure the necklace around her neck. There was little doubt that the earl would approve of his lady's generous actions. During their twelve-year marriage, Lord Worrington had proven himself a most indulgent husband.

"Worrington rarely denies my requests," Georgette said, confirming Maura's suspicions. Her aunt laid her cheek affectionately against Maura's. Side by side, the resemblance between aunt and niece was startling, though Maura considered the attributes more flattering on her aunt. They shared the same nose, and almond-shaped eyes. With her parents' thirst for travel, Maura had adopted many of her aunt's mannerisms, such as how Georgette tipped her chin smugly upward when she was confident she was correct, and the coy way she brought the back of her hand up to her lips to stifle her laughter. It always seemed to charm Lord Worrington whenever he observed Maura emulating his lady's actions.

There were differences between them as well. For instance, her aunt shared the same eye color as her mother, a warm medium blue. Maura had inherited her paternal grandmother's eye color, which was a moody sea-gray.

Maura was taller by several inches. Her frame was pleasantly formed, but nature had been slightly generous, rounding her hips and bosom. Georgette was slender, and often lamented that her bodice would benefit from some plumpness in her bosom.

Both possessed tresses with a natural tendency to curl. However, Maura's hair was a rich brown with a hint of a ripe strawberry hue, while Georgette's thinner shoulder-length tresses were light brown. When Maura was a child, it had been her fervent desire to grow up into the renowned beauty her aunt was.

In truth, she wanted Georgette to be her mother.

The only child of Lord and Lady Courtwill, she had been born of older parents who had little interest in having a child. They were both respected scientists, and their intellectual pursuits had made them soul mates. There was little time for rearing an unwanted child. How disappointing it must have been for her parents when they realized that they had not even managed to produce an heir.

For reasons Maura could not divine, Georgette had taken pity on her sister's lonely daughter. Lord and Lady Courtwill traveled extensively, and Georgette made certain there was always a place for Maura in her household. Georgette was not a paragon of motherhood. After all, there were balls to attend, evenings at the theater, and handsome scoundrels to charm. A governess and the household servants watched over Maura while her aunt enjoyed her adventures.

When Georgette returned, she lavished her niece with attention and humorous stories. In her aunt's household, Maura felt like she had a place. Oh, she loved her parents. In their own way, they returned her affection. They gave her an enviable education for a nobleman's daughter and clothed and fed her. On one or two occasions, she even joined them on one of their research journeys.

And yet, Maura owed her aunt everything. Georgette had recognized a kindred spirit in the lonely child, and had openly embraced her. She had filled Maura's dreary childhood with affection, escapades, and laughter.

Only once, a little more than twelve years ago, her aunt had reminded Maura of her debt.

As a result, someone else had paid a high price for Maura's loyalty.

"Why the frown?" Georgette playfully pinched her niece's cheek. "Still fussing about the necklace, are you? Well, if all goes according to plan, the necklace will remain in the Worrington family."

Ah, yes, Mr. Rowan Lidsaw. He was the second son of Lord Worrington, and the man's current favorite. He was three years older than Maura, and she had known him since they were children. When he was not away at school, he had been her confidant and amiable companion who entertained her at Worrington Hall. Since she had turned sixteen, the earl and her aunt had hinted that a match between the pair would be warmly welcomed. Maura should have suspected when she had agreed to join her aunt and uncle in London that Rowan would be included in their romantic machinations.

"Do you ever cease playing matchmaker, Aunt?" Maura said, exasperated by the subject. She rolled her eyes and stepped away from the looking glass. "Rowan is a fine gentleman, and a considerate friend. Nevertheless, he has not begged for my hand or heart. If you have invited me to London so you and the earl can bully poor Rowan into declaring himself, you might as well order a coach so I may return home."

"And miss London?" Georgette taunted lightly, sensing her niece was anticipating the trip as much as she was. "Why would you want to spend the season in seclusion when you could be visiting museums, attending lectures, balls, card parties—"

Exasperated, Maura raised her hands in a surrendering gesture. "Enough! Your argument is sound. I would be a fool to refuse such a generous invitation."

Feeling a whisper of melancholy, she sank into the nearest chair. How could she explain to her aunt that the notion of being leg-shackled to Rowan dimmed the adventure of visiting London? With Rowan at her side, she might as well already be married. She would not be whiling her nights away dancing till dawn, or coyly flirting with mysterious gentlemen from a theater box. At two and twenty, most ladies her age had enjoyed numerous seasons. Many had already married and birthed their husband's heir. Lord and Lady Courtwill had been too distracted by their scientific pursuits to bother with something as trite as introducing their only daughter to the *ton*. It was an oversight that Georgette clearly intended to correct.

"Your sadness tears at my heart." Her aunt knelt at Maura's feet. "While Worrington and I would like nothing better than for you and Rowan to announce your betrothal, I understand a young lady's heart. You are young, beautiful, and possess the wealth to indulge your whims. You want not just one gentleman to worship you; you desire all of London to bow at your feet."

Maura giggled at the outrageous suggestion. "Really, Aunt—"

Georgette touched her finger to Maura's lips. "You crave romance. A courtship. No, do not deny it. What lady wants to be bound to a gentleman who has not taken the time to woo her? You are innocence and ripe passion. You deserve to experience the gentle seduction of love poetry and small tokens of affection. To feel the excitement of a lover's unguarded stare across a crowded ballroom, or taste the sweetness of a stolen kiss in the shadows of a garden."

Her aunt used the back of the chair to rise slowly from her cramped position. She placed the palm of her hand on the small of her back. "Rowan has been remiss in courting you properly, and perhaps your uncle and I are to blame. A conquest easily won is never prized as the battle almost lost. Besides, if my stepson cannot withstand a little competition for your heart, then he is undeserving of my niece."

Maura jumped up from her seat and embraced Georgette. Her aunt was a complicated mix of ambition and generosity. When provoked, she could be a formidable enemy. It was a lesson Maura had never forgotten. However, it was appreciation for Georgette's insight and kindness that overwhelmed Maura. "You must think I am an ungrateful wretch for wanting more, when you and Worrington have given me so much."

"Not at all. I want you to be happy, little girl," Georgette murmured into Maura's hair. "Besides, I think you underestimate Rowan's interest. I predict you will lead him on a merry chase this season!"

Satisfied that Maura's fears had been eased, Georgette deftly changed the subject back to their earlier discussion of what jewelry should be taken to London. As her aunt displayed the Worrington emeralds, Maura privately wondered if Georgette had considered that their trip to town would bring them into Everod's realm. Worrington's heir would not be pleased when he learned of their arrival. Maura could only pray that the gentleman's thirst for revenge had waned over the twelve years of silence.

CHAPTER 2

"Evenings with *les sauvages nobles* have become positively mundane," Everod proclaimed as he sipped brandy in Ramscar's town house.

In spite of his sarcasm, he had enjoyed the evening with his friends. Their little gatherings had grown over the years to include Solitea's and Ramscar's wives. The duchess's ten-year-old sister, Gypsy, had also joined them this evening. When he first had encountered the girl two years earlier, she had been mute. At the time, it appeared her fragile mind had been damaged by the sudden loss of her parents, and the cruelty of her abusive older brother. Now that she and her sister Kilby were under Solitea's protection, little Gypsy had gradually become a veritable chatterbox.

Their supper had been excellent, and the conversation stimulating. Still, there had been an unspoken tension hidden beneath their joviality. On several occasions, Everod had noticed a look of concern pass between Solitea and his duchess. Kilby had almost seemed relieved when Ramscar had proposed that the gentlemen continue their friendly arguments in his library where the earl had amassed a collection of antique weapons that would have impressed Nelson.

Sipping his brandy, Everod lazily watched as his host crouched down to tend the coals in the fireplace. Solitea, their designated leader, leaned negligibly against the mantel observing their friend's efforts. Edgy, Cadd had separated himself from the others and stared broodingly out the open window of Ramscar's library.

"I suppose we could abandon the ladies and pay our respects to Moirai's Lust," Solitea said, referring to a gambling hell that was owned by one of his brother-in-law's friends. "Kilby will understand."

Cadd snorted in grim amusement. "Your duchess is likely to sever your bollocks, and Ram's lady, Patience, would ask your butler Scrimm for one of Cook's dullest knives. Ladies have a peculiar notion where a respectable married gent should dally. A notorious hell is not one of them."

Solitea laughed, shaking his head. "Since when have you become an expert on the workings of a lady's mind?"

"I never claimed to be," Cadd retorted, stepping away from the window to join them. "What man can breach such a thorny citadel? However, I have had the sincere pleasure of observing you pathetic rogues bumble your way to wedded bliss."

"Needless to say, both Cadd and I have been extremely amused by your errors and confusion," Everod cheerfully added as he glanced over his shoulder and saluted Cadd with his glass of brandy.

"And let us not forget the substantial profits gained." Cadd clinked his glass against Everod's, and winked.

"When will the pair of you learn that I despise

having my personal business reduced to petty wagers?" Solitea nodded at Ramscar. "What say you, Ram? Should we take them into the gardens and thrash some sense into these scoundrels?"

Ramscar sighed wearily as he rose from his haunches. "It hasn't done us much good in the past. However, if you are looking for a fair fight, I am willing."

Although he was shorter, Ramscar's skill with weapons was renowned. Only a fool would believe he was getting a fair fight when the earl was his opponent. "While the notion of seeing Cadd's pretty face pummeled sounds tempting," Everod drawled, his steady gaze studying Solitea's mildly inquisitive expression, "I think we should first discuss the actual reason we were summoned for supper this evening."

"Everod, what the devil are you blathering about?" Cadd demanded. He grabbed the full decanter of brandy on the table and began refilling everyone's glasses.

"Call it instinct, but something is afoot, my friend." Everod carelessly gestured at Solitea. "He and his lady have been exchanging somber looks all evening."

The marquess brushed back the dark brown lock of hair that obscured his vision. "Solitea probably angered his duchess. So how long has it been since she allowed you into her bed?"

"Who says I need a bed to please my lady?" Solitea fired back, though it was obvious he was enjoying the banter.

"I doubt your duchess would be pleased if she knew of this discussion," Ramscar, always the bloody peacemaker, quietly reminded them.

"Really, Cadd. How very provincial of you!" Everod taunted for good measure. The twenty-five-year-old marquess was so easily provoked. "When you find a lady who can tolerate you, I will show you how to pleasure her properly."

"Condescending arse!" Cadd muttered under his breath. "I've noticed your lovers never linger after they've endured your clumsy fumbles."

Everod jumped to his feet, and gave his friend a cocky grin. "They stay long enough for me to satisfy both our needs. And what of your bawdy adventures, my friend? Pray tell us, when was the last time you had a soft, willing female beneath you? Or are males your preference these days?"

From Cadd's outraged expression, Everod knew he had pushed his friend beyond the limit. Before he could apologize, the marquess shoved him backward, sending him crashing into a table. The four legs of the delicate table exploded with the burden of Everod's weight.

"Enough!" Ramscar roared, and charged at both struggling men. Cadd landed a blow to Everod's gut before Solitea dragged the man away.

"A bit tardy, old man," Everod said, wincing slightly as he tested the tenderness of his stomach with his fingers.

Shaking his head with disgust, Ramscar offered Everod his hand. "Baiting Cadd will not get you the answers you seek."

"True. However, waiting for you and Solitea to come to the point was just getting tiresome." Everod grimaced as he straightened his spine. He glanced derisively at the table, which had splintered into expensive kindling. "It appears I owe you a new table."

"And me, a damn apology," Cadd interjected. He shook off Solitea's firm grip.

"It is unimportant," the earl assured Everod. Crossing his arms, he looked from one man to the other. "Have both of you finished?"

Everod was tempted to deliver a sarcastic response, but he heeded Solitea's silent warning and held his tongue. Cadd was still riled, but he remained silent. That did not prevent him from taking every opportunity to glare at him. They had been friends since they were young boys, and the occasional bloodied nose or bruised pride was their equivalent of affection. In truth, he loved the marquess like a brother. Once his temper waned, all would be forgiven until their next scuffle.

"After dealing with you jackanapes, raising the Carlisle heir should be as simple as breathing," Solitea said. He bent down and retrieved Cadd's glass from the floor and placed it beside the decanter.

"If I recall, your mother described you as a devilish handful," Everod said, settling back down onto the sofa. "The old duke was so proud."

"Speaking of family . . ." Ramscar said, giving Solitea a meaningful stare.

Everod closed his eyes and muttered a silent oath. The rumors about Lord and Lady Worrington's arrival in town had already reached his friends' ears. "I would rather not. The subject is tedious at best."

"Bloody hell, old Worrington is in town, isn't he?" Cadd guessed, his tone ripe with disgust as his loyalty to Everod eclipsed his ire.

"Yes. My mother encountered Lord and Lady Worrington at a soiree, and considering the bad blood between you and your father, she thought you should be warned." Solitea studied Everod's face. "You already knew."

"Solitea, please pass along my gratitude to your mother," Everod said mildly. "Do you think she would accept a small gift as a token of my appreciation?"

The duke grimaced. "Invariably. However, a note will suffice. Sending the duchess gifts will only encourage the lady to meddle in your life."

"Or create a situation in which Solitea will be forced to murder you," Ramscar muttered from behind him.

Even before the death of her beloved duke, the dowager duchess was renowned for taking lovers twenty years her junior. Everod had also garnered a certain reputation for seducing any lady who crossed his path. Although he thought the dowager duchess was a charming and beautiful woman, Everod knew he would be risking his life if he courted anything more than maternal concern from Solitea's mother.

"You worry for naught, Ram." Everod tipped his head back so he could glance at him with one eye. "Truth be told, I am too old for the duchess."

Solitea cleared his throat. "I do not want to hear any more speculation about my mother's preference in male companions," the duke ordered tersely. Despite his rakish ways, Solitea had feelings toward his mother that could be downright traditional. "We were discussing the Worringtons."

Everod finished off his brandy with a hearty swallow. "You were, Solitea, not I. What Worrington does while in town is his business as long as he stays out of mine." He slammed his glass on the side table and leaned forward to rise from the sofa.

Cadd snorted. "Rather charitable of you, Everod, since the old man did his best to sever your head from your throat."

If Everod thought about it, he could still recall the moment when his father's blade bit into the tender flesh of his neck, the warm spray of his blood as it coated his face and chest, and his life measured in heartbeats until the damage could be repaired. He never spoke to anyone about those long hours when terror and pain dominated his thoughts those first days after his father's attack when he was certain he would die.

His mocking expression did not betray his darker thoughts. "Well, I didn't say I was intending to kiss the man! If Worrington has any sense, he should know that twelve years has made me a little wiser, and a thousand times meaner."

Last time, guilt and shame had stayed Everod's hand. He had deserved his father's anger. What Everod could never forgive was the fact that Worrington believed his wife's lies about his elder son. He had aligned himself with that treacherous whore, while Everod had been banished and forgotten.

Well, mayhap not forgotten entirely.

If his informants were correct, Miss Maura Keighly was currently residing in Worrington's town house. Everod wondered if she thought of him on occasion.

He had not forgotten her.

Solitea stirred from his perch, obviously not satisfied with Everod's response. "My friend, the man is your father. Perhaps his arrival heralds a chance for you and Worrington to heal old wounds."

Everod idly rubbed part of the scarring near his left ear. "Some wounds never fully heal." He held up a silencing hand before the duke could argue. "Regardless, I have no intention of provoking a confrontation with my father, so the three of you can stop looking so worried. I have no interest in gaining Worrington's favor, and his title and wealth will be mine with patience."

Of course, Maura Keighly was not family.

Lost in thought, Everod stared into the bottom of his empty glass. Maura had been a mere girl when he had been forcibly escorted from Worrington Hall and banished forever. A beautiful child, it was reasonable to assume Maura had grown into an alluring woman.

Like Georgette.

The bitter thought hardened Everod's resolve.

He had been used by one beautiful bitch and callously discarded. He would not allow his memories of a child with sea-gray eyes to soften him. Why not use Maura Keighly to exact his revenge? It would be the last ploy Georgette would anticipate. While the lady fretted about his presence in London, Everod would be giving her precious niece the thorough fucking she deserved for the lies she had uttered to protect her aunt. There was a sweet symmetry to his plan.

Everod tapped his knuckle against the glass in anticipation.

There was no reason to limit his revenge to one night of seduction. He could spend weeks sating his lust and his revenge within her tight, willing body.

He possessed the skill to ensure that she enjoyed it.

It might be entertaining to seduce Maura Keighly so utterly that she was a willing accomplice in her own downfall.

CHAPTER 3
April 4, 1811, London

"I am having second thoughts about the pink trim on the bonnet," Georgette said to Maura as they stood near their carriage, already overburdened with the purchases they had made their first afternoon in London. "Pink was never a color I favored overly much. I think the light green would be a better choice."

Maura softly groaned. They had patronized every shop on Bond Street, and frankly, she was exhausted. She was hungry, and her feet ached. In contrast, her aunt seemed to be invigorated by the bustling activity around her. As long as Worrington's credit was good, Georgette had the stamina to spend his wealth.

"If you are undecided, Aunt, why not order both colors? After all, I heard the earl tell you that he wanted you to be happy," Maura reminded the countess.

"Why not? And if the pink does not please me, then I shall give it to you," Georgette said, pleased that the matter was so easily settled. "Come along."

"No," Maura said sharply, causing her aunt to give her a measured stare. "If you do not mind, I would like to continue up the street. There was a bookseller . . ."

Georgette grimaced, and held a hand up in surrender. "Say no more." Her aunt was a lady who chose to participate in adventures, instead of reading about them in an old dusty tome. "I bring you to London, and you want to look at books. Heavens, you are more like your insipid mother than you might believe."

The casual insult was delivered with such keen precision that Maura did not feel the sting of it until Georgette had moved on to other matters.

"Off with you." Her aunt adjusted her parasol to keep the sunlight from tanning her face. "I will return to the shop and place my order for the green bonnet while you peruse the bookseller's stalls. We will meet again at the carriage."

Maura watched as a footman chased after his mistress. Shrugging elegantly at her aunt's dismissal, she pivoted and strolled away in the opposite direction. The walkway was crowded with pedestrians, a mix of the fashionable and those who were plying their trade. Street vendors sang out while the sounds of horses and their equipage rattled and clanged as the traffic rumbled down the street.

Maura had been to London before with her parents. They had presented their papers to the scientific peers and given lectures to the intellectual elite over the years. Polite society, however, was deemed unimportant so Lord and Lady Courtwill rarely visited London during the height of the social season.

Approaching one of the tables placed just outside the door of the bookseller's shop, Maura nodded to the young gentleman who was clearly guarding the books stacked on the table. She picked up a thin green tome and frowned at the worn stitching on the spine. Maura set the book down, and inspected several others. Most of the books were damaged. It was apparent the book-seller had purchased the inferior contents of a gentle-man's library, and was attempting to recoup his losses. Giving up on the outdoor tables, Maura stepped inside the shop in the hopes of purchasing a book worthy of its price.

Caught up in her inspection of the discounted books, she had not sensed that her actions were been scrutinized from afar. When Maura walked into the bookseller's shop, Everod agilely dodged the street traffic crossing his path, and with cool determination, he followed her inside.

So the rumors were true, after all. She dared to enter his town.

Although twelve years had passed, Everod would have recognized Maura Keighly even if she had not been standing next to his cunning stepmother. The engaging girl who had become entangled in his night-mares had bloomed into a striking young lady.

Everod smiled at his good fortune.

Bedding this traitorous beauty would be no hardship. If a man could make a list of his perfect female, Maura Keighly physically met all of his requirements. Her pale oval face with its defined cheekbones and straight nose were balanced with expressive sea-gray eyes and ruby lips ripe for kissing.

Over the years, her lanky girlish frame had elon-gated, and Maura had matured into a dominating height of femininity. His hungry gaze mentally stripped away her cumbersome skirts and it was simple for him to imagine the long, firm legs hidden from him like a wrapped present. He almost groaned out loud at the thought of her legs constricting him as he shoved his cock into her. His six-feet-and-three-inch unyielding frame of bone and muscle usually overwhelmed most of his lovers. Maura could handle him. Everod would not have to be gentle with her.

Christ, his body was already humming in anticipation. Just the thought of placing his bare hands on the gentle curves of her hips and hauling her soft buttocks against him was making him edgy. Everod slowed his gait as he tried to control his visceral response to Maura. Tiny beads of sweat were forming on his forehead, and he had not even introduced himself!

Completely unaware of his lustful perusal, she smiled absently at two gentlemen before she moved past them to scrutinize a wall of books. The two young bucks nudged and murmured to each other, both willing to play flirtatious games with the pretty stranger. Everod felt a surge of triumph as Maura's disinterest doused their lustful hopes.

The lady is mine, gents!

Disappointed, the two gentlemen walked out the door.

Presented with her back, Everod admired her willowy frame. She was tall for a female. He imagined the top of her head would reach his collarbone.

Murmuring something unintelligible, Maura glided to the right as he moved in closer. She was attired in a plain cambric morning dress with a short train that consisted of three rows of ruffles. A mantle of French gray satin was fastened to her right shoulder with some sort of brooch. A white unbleached al fresco chip hat obscured her face and dark hair as she reached up on her tiptoes and removed a book from the shelf.

Everod wondered if Maura ever thought of him, and the vital role she had played in his banishment from the family. Over the years, he had made a point of keeping track of his family and Maura Keighly's summer visits to Worrington Hall. With indifferent parents, the lady had developed a loving relationship with her aunt. A self-proclaimed cynic, Everod believed the scheming Lady Worrington and her niece were not finished with the Lidsaw men. Seeing them together, he viewed them as formidable enemies, but now they were in his domain.

He knew, almost to the day, when his father was planning to bring the family and Maura Keighly to London for the season. The earl might have dismissed his elder son; however, Everod had spies in the Worrington household. He had been quietly collecting information about his family for years.

Twelve years ago, his clash with his stepmother and Maura Keighly had been on their terms. Everod was older, wiser in some ways, and he had learned how to handle ambitious ladies who were willing to whore themselves to get what they wanted. Unbeknownst to Maura, any games between them would be played by *his* rules.

Perhaps it was time to let Maura know her diminutive place in his world. Moving stealthily up from behind, Everod peered over Maura's shoulder to glimpse the tome that seemed to captivate her. Reading a few lines of text, he bent down and whispered into her ear, "Still the romantic, I see. I would have assumed Georgette would have snuffed such a whimsical inclination."

Startled by the gentleman's unsettling proximity, Maura snapped the book shut and whirled away from the masculine lips that had casually brushed the outer scroll of her ear. She backed up and belatedly realized that there was no escape. With the book clutched like a shield to her breast, Maura sputtered several syllables of unintelligible outrage. It was only when she dared to meet the stranger's gaze that she realized the gentleman was not unfamiliar to her.

And he knew Georgette.

Everod.

Oh God. Was it truly him? Maura was so shaken by his presence that she unconsciously reached out and touched his arm. The solid muscle of his forearm jerked under her fingers as if the brazen contact had startled the viscount, too. Their eyes met, but she was the first to look away.

Still, the image of his uncompromising handsome face was burned into her memory. One glance had banished the boy, and replaced him with the towering man who had a face that radiated both virility and power. She had felt the weight of his amber-green gaze as he scrutinized her face. Satisfaction had flared in his eyes. Her instinctive fear had pleased him. His black hair was longer than she remembered. The glossy black length was bound in a short queue. With his lips firmly pressed together, he reminded her of a hardened warrior.

As she withdrew her hand, she offered him a hesitant smile. "Lord Everod, I suppose it was inevitable that we would meet again."

Injured and filled with rage, the sixteen-year-old Everod had delivered the vow that they would meet again like a threat. Maura had believed him then. Even if she had not, the intimidating man standing before her now was fully capable of carrying out the revenge that had been denied him twelve years earlier.

"Miss Keighly," his low voice rumbled like thunder in her ears. "I did not mean to frighten you."

Liar. There was no reason for her to believe that he had planned this encounter. However, Everod had seized the opportunity to gain the upper hand. She felt unsettled and vulnerable, and the blackguard knew it.

"I was not frightened," she said, her heart pounding in her chest. He grinned, and Maura was not fooled for a moment that amusement prompted his friendly response. "Flustered," she hastily amended. It was madness to confess to a man like Everod that the first response he had stirred in her was fear. "You merely flustered me. I was lost in thought, and did not anticipate—"

"Either friend or foe?" he politely supplied, when words failed her muddled brain.

The young girl who recalled the angry young lord who had craved revenge wanted to edge away from him, and cry out to the patrons of the establishment for their protection. There was something in his expression that stalled her retreat. Everod expected her to run. No, he hoped that she would run! Still hugging the forgotten book, Maura held the viscount's unwavering gaze and slowly dipped into a respectful curtsy to acknowledge his noble status.

"Lord Everod, your presence is unexpected, but not unwelcome," she softly lied. "Forgive me for not recognizing you immediately. It has been many years since we last met." Maura mentally cringed at her inane remark. So much for her pathetic attempt at polite conversation. There was no need to remind the viscount that at their last meeting, his father had ordered his seriously injured son from Worrington Hall.

"Twelve to be precise," he said succinctly. Everod braced his palm against the bookcase behind her as if to discourage any thoughts of flight. "I recognized you immediately."

There was a fluttering sensation in her abdomen as she digested the certainty in his inflection. Since she had been a mere ten at the time, it seemed a trifle disturbing that he could pick her out of a crowd so readily. Perhaps it was his confidence that ruffled her feminine pride. She would like to believe that he no longer saw the face of a child when he gazed at her.

No, that was not quite the truth.

She did not want Lord Everod to see the young girl who had betrayed him all those years ago.

"While flattering, my lord, I find it difficult to believe," she said in a brisk tone as she turned slightly and slid the book she had been reading before Everod's interruption into the narrow space on the shelf.

In spite of her words, Maura quietly conceded it had only taken a moment for her to identify the tall handsome stranger who had startled her. Time and distance had blurred his features, except for his eyes.

Unique and haunting, his eyes were light amber with outer and inner rings of dark green. Twelve years ago, she had seen them with an inner fire of injustice and hatred. This afternoon they glowed with a cold cynical amusement. Her face and throat burned under his intense scrutiny.

"Are you calling me a liar, Miss Keighly?"

Everod had tossed the accusation out as bluntly as another man might have issued a challenge. The question felt like a blow to her cheek, because once her silence had called him a liar.

He had evidently not forgiven her or forgotten.

Maura's gaze unwillingly sought out the scar she glimpsed on the right underside of his jaw when he cocked his head. The fancy knot of his cravat covered most of his throat; however, she knew what the starched linen concealed. A long wicked scar of dishonor. It began on the left side of his neck and curved around until it disappeared on the right underside of his jawbone. With the exception of his mistresses, Maura doubted many had seen his scar, and few still were brave enough to question its origin.

"Come, Miss Keighly, I shall not be offended by the truth," he taunted softly. "Am I a liar?"

The viscount was clever with words. He spoke of past and present in the same breath. It was enough to muddle her brain. "No, my lord. I would never call you a liar." She gave him an inscrutable look. "Regardless, my opinion is of no importance."

"Do not belittle yourself." He moved in closer and his proximity forced her to lower her gaze. "Your fine opinion carries weight with my sire, my family."

Maura touched her stomach, half expecting to find his blade buried to the hilt. She had to admire his skill. His double-edged words were razor sharp and his delivery almost effortless. "You misunderstood me, Lord Everod. I was referring to the here and now. I knew you when you were barely a man."

"Now you insult me!" he said, laughing at her explanation.

"And you are being intentionally obtuse. I doubt you would have heeded any advice from your fifteen-year-old self," she said, her frustration increasing as he twisted her words to his liking. "You are seven and twenty. I confess, I do not know the gentleman you have become."

She took a bold step forward, intending to walk by him. With luck, she might even make it out the door unmolested. Everod's hand shot out and clamped onto her elbow. Maura did not test the strength of his hold. She was certain he would not release her until he was finished with her.

Everod stared down at his gloved hand on her arm. "Have you not forgotten something?"

"What do you want? An apology?" she asked, unable to quell the defensiveness and rising panic in her voice. Twelve years had not eased her shame. It burned and bubbled like acid in her belly. "You have it. A day has not passed when I have not—"

"Spare me, your heartfelt sentiment," he said brusquely. "If a simple apology would have satisfied me, I would have already claimed it."

Maura trembled. What did Everod want from her?

Revenge? She silently acknowledged that she deserved his disdain. If she had not summoned Worrington after finding Everod with her aunt, the earl might have never learned of their betrayal. Her impetuous actions had cost Everod to forfeit almost everything, including his life. Regret did not even begin to describe her feelings.

On the other hand, Everod was not willing to forgive anyone.

Maura needed to get away from him.

Standing so close to him that she could smell the enticing scent of soap and man was confusing her. The child in her wanted to run away, and find her aunt. The woman in her wanted to remain, and challenge him in an attempt to learn more about the man Everod had become. "Then I would not presume to bore you with my apology. What do you want?"

He grinned irreverently at her frosty tone. "Radcliffe's *In a Sicilian Romance*. You were thoroughly enthralled with the tale until I intruded. Were you intending to purchase both volumes?"

Maura had forgotten all about the books. Ann Radcliffe's gothic tale would have to wait till another day. She had no intention of lingering a second longer than she had to with Everod watching her. "No. I was just admiring the workmanship."

Everod looked unconvinced. "If you do not have the funds, I could purchase them—"

Something akin to horror crept into her expression. "No! I mean, no, thank you, my lord. That will be unnecessary." Maura stared pointedly at his hand on her arm. She took a deep fortifying breath when he released her. "I have tarried here too long. I—the carriage awaits me." She thought it best not to mention her aunt to the viscount.

"Very well. I will not keep you." He surprised her by capturing her hand and bowing gallantly. Maura felt the warmth of his lips through her kid gloves as he pressed a kiss onto her knuckles.

Recalling her own manners, she dipped into an abbreviated curtsy. "Good day, my lord." She hesitated. "If you like, I will send your father your warm regards," she offered with feigned nonchalance, as it suddenly occured to her that Everod might have approached her in an attempt to heal the breach between him and his father.

Any hope she might have harbored in her heart was ruthlessly crushed. The warmth she had glimpsed in his handsome face vanished. "I do not recall offering them, Miss Keighly."

The Lidsaw males were a stubborn, unforgiving lot. Maura nodded. "Then I would be foolish to pretend otherwise."

She started for the door.

"Miss Keighly?"

Maura halted and tilted her head questioningly at the viscount. "Was there something else, my lord?"

With a casual stride he caught up to her. "Yes, I believe there is. I want you to ponder something on your drive home with that bitch you call your aunt beside you."

"Yes?"

"You claimed not to know the gentleman I have

become at seven and twenty." He towered over her, using his height and closeness to his advantage. "I have decided to resolve your quandary."

Maura did not like the gleeful manner in which the viscount's eyes glimmered as he stared down at her puzzled expression. "I do not quite understand, Lord Everod."

He brushed his thumb over the fine bones of her hand. Until now, she had not realized that he had not relinquished her hand. "You are in my territory, Miss Keighly. My rules," Everod said, his somber proclamation prickling the invisible hairs on the back of her neck. "By season's end, you will not be able to make the same innocent claim."

One of the servants told me that you requested a tray," Georgette said, glancing back at her while her aunt's personal maid fastened the back of her dress. "Are you ill, child?"

Maura had said very little to Georgette since she had dashed to the Worringtons' carriage as if the devil had been at her heels.

Literally.

She supposed there was some truth to her fanciful imagery. Lord Everod could never be mistaken for a saint.

"Forgive me, Aunt, but I must cry off from joining you and Uncle this evening. I confess, I have been feeling unwell. If you do not mind, I would like to retire early this evening."

Georgette turned around. Crossing her arms, she gave Maura an aggrieved look. "This is a dreadful time for you to be ill. Rowan was hoping to spend part of his evening with us."

"Of course, you will extend my apologies to him as well," Maura demurely replied.

She had not told her aunt about her encounter with Everod.

When Maura had left the bookseller's, she had had every intention of warning Georgette that the viscount had sought her out. There was old business between the three of them, and Everod did not impress her as the forgiving sort. Nor was Georgette to be underestimated. Maura had learned after Everod's banishment that her beloved aunt had not been entirely truthful in regard to her tryst with her stepson. Twelve years ago Maura's loyalties had been torn. Her brief meeting with the viscount proved that time had not improved her thorny predicament.

"Are you feverish?" With a slight frown creasing her brow, Georgette took a step toward her niece. She brought a finely embroidered handkerchief up to her nose to avoid coming down with the ailment, too.

"No, Aunt. Just a minor stomach complaint." Maura closed her eyes as her aunt's cool fingers pressed against her cheek.

"I disagree. You do feel feverish." Georgette backed away from Maura. "Oh, dear. You must take to your bed immediately. I will have Cook send up one of my special teas that will help ease your discomfort. Worrington will be so disappointed that you won't be joining us this evening."

Dismissing her niece, Georgette returned her attention to the cosmetics on her dressing table. She had to prepare herself for the evening out. Although Maura knew her aunt loved her, Georgette's interest in anything other than herself was rather limited.

"Good evening, Aunt. You will send Uncle and Rowan my regrets?"

"Yes . . . yes," Georgette said absently.

Maura quietly slipped out of her aunt's bedchamber, allowing another opportunity to warn her aunt about her stepson to fade away.

She had little doubt that Lord Everod would soon reveal himself to Lord and Lady Worrington. If they intended to declare war on each other, Maura was not going to place herself between them.

Or be anyone's pawn.

Ever again.

CHAPTER 4

"B y God, I should kill you for your insult!" Everod roared. He sucked air through his clenched teeth as a painful cramp rippled through his abdomen.

Untroubled by the viscount's rage, his cherub-faced attacker grinned impenitently down at him. The boy was not even two years old, and he had bested a man who had recently celebrated his twenty-seventh birthday. It was utterly humiliating.

Everod's seething gaze settled on the child's sire, who strolled over to rescue his son. "Brawley, if you value this fiendish imp, you will remove him from my sight!" he snapped, the white of his teeth flashing in warning.

Maccus Brawley plucked his son out of Everod's hands, and neatly passed the gleeful child over to his wife, Lady Fayre. Everod's eyes narrowed when he noted that the lady attempted to muffle her laughter under the guise of hugging the boy.

Fighting back his own laughter, Brawley rubbed his jaw. "My apologies, Everod. And my sympathies. Stomping on a gent's cods is a new game for young Derek. One we cannot seem to discourage."

"Well, what do you expect with Carlisle blood

running in the boy's veins? Born fighters, the lot of them," Curling his hand into a fist, Everod resisted the need to cup his abused groin in front of the two ladies present, the young Duchess of Solitea and her sister-in-law, Lady Fayre. Instead, he pressed his fisted hand into his left thigh and tried not to gag.

Fayne Carlisle, Duke of Solitea, felt no compunction about laughing at his friend's discomfort. Everod shot a quelling glance in his direction.

"You are cruel to laugh at poor Everod." Fayne's duchess came to his defense. "Derek managed to kick the butler and two footmen this morning. Hedge has not spoken a civil word to anyone since the unfortunate incident."

"Why do you think I insisted that our man Everod be the one to hold the frisky rascal," Solitea said, completely unrepentant. "With luck, the boy will outgrow his game before it is my turn to amuse him."

Everod made a rude noise. "Solitea, your generosity knows no bounds. Any hopes that I might father an heir one day was likely quashed with one impressive kick."

Lady Fayre made a sympathetic sound. "Does it hurt overly much, Everod?"

Everod responded to her asinine query with a growl. Brawley and Solitea laughed, but he noted the silent commiserating exchange between the two men regarding his injury.

His brief exchange with Maura Keighly had prompted him to accept Solitea's offer to spend a quiet evening with the Carlisle family. It only took an hour for Everod to regret his decision. Now happily married to his duchess, his friend had recommended an evening of restraint to counter the whirlwind of reck-less living the social season in London always incited.

It was a damn shame to listen to one of London's most licentious rakes lecture *him* on restraint. Years earlier, he, Solitea, then known simply as Carlisle, Ramscar, and Cadd had eschewed the shackles of re-sponsibility and roamed London with the sole purpose of creating their own amusements. The *ton* had dubbed the four *les sauvages nobles,* or the noble savages.

It was a nickname that suited them perfectly, or had until two of his friends had lost their heads and mar-ried. Solitea had been the first of their group to suc-cumb to Cupid's arrow. Not even the suspicion that his lady might have been his own father's mistress had de-terred his friend from surrendering to the coy wiles of Lady Kilby Fitchwolf.

A year later, their friend Fowler Knowden, Earl of Ramscar, fell hard for a little curvaceous blonde by the name of Miss Patience Farnaly. Everod might have laughed aloud at his once sensible friend's leg-shackled predicament if the situation had not been so heartbreaking.

Everod meant no disrespect to his friends' wives. He felt nothing but a growing admiration and affec-tion for both women. However, the days when the *ton* had anticipated the excitement and mischief of *les sauvages nobles* were fading into banality. Perhaps Solitea and Ramscar did not mourn the loss of their freedom. Even Maccus Brawley, who had married Solitea's younger sister, Lady Fayre, seemed content in his marriage. So that left he and Cadd to carry on the tradition without their friends.

Of course, these days Cadd could no longer be counted on. He had been behaving damned odd, even for him!

"Well, since Derek has ruined your sense of humor," Lady Fayre said, her green eyes sparkling with suppressed humor, "I shall take him upstairs to his nurse."

Kilby, Solitea's demure, dark-haired duchess, abruptly rose at her sister-in-law's announcement. As a sign of respect, all three gentlemen stood. "I will join you, Fayre. Our absence will give the men some time to cheer Everod out of his sulks."

"I am not sulking," Everod muttered.

The duchess opened her arms to Derek in silent invitation. The boy eagerly reached for his aunt, and wrapped his arms around her neck.

Something about the affectionate exchange prompted Everod to ask, "So, little duchess, when are you getting down to the business of giving Solitea here his own cods-stomping heir?"

It was an extraordinarily rude question, even for a close friend of the family. Everod subtly braced himself, half expecting Solitea to smack him on the back of the head for his outrageous behavior.

Composed, the young duchess merely arched her right brow at his impertinent question. Her lips curled into an arrogant smirk. "Who says I haven't, Everod?" Satisfied with his stunned expression, Kilby strolled off with her precious burden while a laughing Lady Fayre followed just a step behind her.

Everod glanced at Solitea. From his friend's indulgent expression and Brawley's amusement as the men watched the two women disappear through the doorway, it was apparent the duchess's announcement had not been a surprise.

Grinning, Everod clapped his friend on the back. "Solitea, I see congratulations are in order. Did I happen to mention that Cadd and I have a long-standing wager on your fertility or lack thereof?"

Solitea gave him an aggrieved look. "Are you and Cadd void of all scruples? Is nothing sacred?"

Everod offered him a mocking smile. "Apparently not."

Now that the ladies had left the room, Brawley retrieved the brandy from a silver tray along with three glasses. "Your good news calls for something stronger than tea, and a proper toast."

He accepted the glass of brandy Brawley offered him. "To your cock, Solitea," Everod said, ignoring the other man's snort of disbelief. "We are all pleased it is not as empty as your threats."

Solitea tackled him before Everod could bring the glass of brandy to his lips. He flung his hand out as he and Solitea landed halfway on the sofa. Everod heard the glass shatter behind them. Laughing, he barely felt the punch Solitea landed on his stomach. Though to be fair, his friend was more exasperated than angry with him. If Solitea had wanted to make an impression with his fist, the man had the skill to deliver his displeasure.

Solitea seized him by the coat and hauled him onto the sofa. The duke was laughing when he pushed Everod into the cushion. "Damn puppy!"

"We're the same age," Everod replied, panting from

their brief fierce exertion. Good-naturedly, he rubbed his abdomen. "Bastard."

"A foul rumor. Likely started by you or Cadd!" Solitea said carelessly as he moved away and accepted Brawley's glass of brandy. He took a healthy swallow. "Christ, Kilby is carrying my child. I am a lucky gent!"

Braced on his elbows, Everod grinned up at his friend. The twist of envy he felt in his gut was likely a mild reaction to Solitea's pathetic excuse for a punch. "I wager you'll swallow those words if your duchess births a girl."

Solitea handed his glass of brandy to Everod, and gave him a level look. "Consider yourself challenged, my friend, if I see my name in the club's betting book. Again!"

Everod took a sip from the glass. Wisely, he refrained from responding.

CHAPTER 5

"My lord, a package has arrived for Miss Keighly," the Worringtons' butler announced shortly after Maura had finished breakfast with her aunt and uncle.

No one was more surprised by the announcement than Maura herself. She had just arrived in town. There had been little time to renew acquaintances, and her parents, while generous, were not the type to send gifts to her when they were traveling.

"Aunt Georgette, are you responsible?" Maura asked, rising and moving to the end of the table where Abbot had placed the mysterious cloth-wrapped gift.

Her aunt shook her head, looking as bemused as Maura felt. "Not I, my precious. My impulsive nature does not complement a well-staged surprise."

The earl chuckled as he reached for his countess's hand. "Very true, my love. However, I adore your impulsiveness."

The trio watched as the butler efficiently cut the cording and unwound the length of waxed fabric protecting the contents.

Maura shifted her gaze to the earl. "What about you, Uncle?"

Lord Worrington gave her an indulgent wink. "I

cannot claim responsibility, little one. It appears our Maura has an admirer."

Rowan.

It was possible. Georgette knew Maura was reluctant about betrothing herself to a gentleman she had viewed as a brother for years. Perhaps the earl and countess had ordered him to court Maura. It was a mortifying thought.

The only thing worse would be that her mysterious admirer was—

"Books. How fascinating," Georgette said without much enthusiasm. She settled back into her chair and signaled for the footman to fill her cup.

Everod.

Maura did not need to peer closely at the two volumes. She recognized the tomes as the very ones she had been admiring at the booksellers. Oh, the arrogance of the madman! What kind of mischief was this? The viscount had to know his package would upset the entire household.

"Is there a card?" the earl inquired politely. Fortunately, he seemed more intent on nibbling his wife's fingers than learning the identity of the sender.

Maura hastily snatched the books up before Abbot could search for the card. "No, Uncle. No card." She opened the first book and snapped it shut. "It appears my admirer prefers to remain anonymous."

"A secret admirer," Lord Worrington mused. "What do you think, my lady, is Rowan teasing our pretty niece?"

Wrong son, Maura dourly thought.

Georgette smiled, the depth of her joy putting a

sparkle in her lovely eyes. Her aunt was determined
to match the young couple, and if Rowan had shown
some creative initiative, then the lady heartily ap-
proved.

"I have noticed for some months that Rowan appears to be enamored with Maura. While I would
have encouraged a slightly more romantic token of
affection, Maura's mysterious admirer has selected a
gift that would please our girl."

With her head full of the knowledge that Everod
was the one who had sent her the books, she needed
to go somewhere private and ponder the viscount's
actions. Was it a brazen taunt? A reminder that his absence had been a matter of choice and that the books
heralded a warning that he was not finished with the
family who had betrayed and abandoned him?

Maura glanced at her aunt and uncle. Her lips relaxed into a faint smile. It was so obvious the earl
loved Georgette. He would do anything for his lady.

*Even if their silent battle ended with Worrington
killing his heir?*

"I have to go," Maura blurted out, her statement
separating the couple. "What I meant is . . . it's a
grand gift!" She backed out toward the door, hugging
the tomes to her chest. "I want to sit somewhere quiet
and read."

She whirled away and slipped out the door Abbot
held open for her. In the distance, Maura could hear
her aunt and uncle's soft laughter at her awkward departure. It was not until she was away from the breakfast room, away from the prying eyes of both family
and staff, that she opened the first volume of *A Sicilian*

Romance by the authoress of *The Castles of Athlin and Dunbayne*.

Lord Everod had taken care not to inscribe anything on the first few pages of the book. After all, anyone might have opened the package, and Maura suspected that any message from the viscount was for her eyes alone. As she thumbed through the pages, a thin piece of paper fluttered out and floated to the marble floor. Maura crouched down to retrieve it. She flipped it over and in a flowing elegant script were three words:

Think of me.

Indeed. The scoundrel knew Maura would do little else until she saw him again.

Everod gently placed his splayed hands over the rounded abdomen of the very pregnant Velouette Whall, Countess of Spryng.

"Good heavens, Vel, how can you bear it? This babe weighs more than you!"

Long ago, before his friend had found his duchess, the widowed countess had been one of the Duke of Solitea's favorite mistresses. Everod had dallied with the lady, too. A few years earlier, there had been a few brief, albeit pleasurable months when Everod had sated himself between the soft generous limbs of Lady Spryng.

Regrettably, he had a faithless heart. That lazy summer he had pursued not only Lady Spryng, but her close friend Lady Silver, and several other silly wenches whose names he could not recall. While Lady Spryng was more tolerant than most women about sharing a lover, she had surprised him one evening by losing her temper. It had been a dreadful row, the sort Everod usually took pains to avoid with his lovers.

Their passionate affair ended that night, but a friendship had taken its place. When he needed a quiet place for reflection or the tender caress of a woman without the messy entanglement of sentiment, he usually found himself sitting in Lady Spryng's boudoir.

Velouette's dark eyes sparkled with humor. "Everod, it is unkind to remind a lady that she has grown so big that she no longer can ascend her carriage!"

Everod grinned unrepentantly up at her. The baby curled within her womb, kicked his hand. The countess gasped and they both laughed at the novelty. Neither one of them had any experience with children. Kissing her belly, Everod rose from his crouched position and sought out one of the nearby chairs in her private parlor.

"Are you feeling well, little mother?" he asked solicitously. "Do you have everything that you need?"

The child was not his. He and Velouette had ended the carnal side of their liaison long before another gent had come along and planted his seed in the young countess. She never spoke of the father. Everod had only asked her once, and the sadness that flashed in her liquid brown gaze prevented him from asking again. Velouette considered the child hers. She was a rich widow, and not without friends. Everod could not help but admire her stubbornness.

"Stop fussing, Everod!" she lightly chided. It was evident that she enjoyed having a friend who worried about her. "I am well. My accoucheur tells me that the babe is growing as he should be."

"So it is a son, you think?"

At six and twenty, the dark-haired Velouette with her rounded figure was an artist's vision of a fertility goddess. Her exotic dusky features were a gift from her Spanish mother. Lord Spryng had claimed her as his countess when she was merely sixteen. Everod could not fault the dead man's taste. Many duels had been fought over the widowed Lady Spryng.

"It would please me to have a son," Velouette said simply with her hands resting on her swollen abdomen. "You know how I enjoy having a male around my house."

Or in her bed.

He immediately doused the thought. That path of meditation would only get him in trouble. "And what of the father, Vel?" Everod silently cursed, wishing he could take back the question when her expression became guarded.

"What of him? He has done enough, do you not think?" she said, her accent becoming more pronounced as her agitation increased. Velouette considered him a close friend, but the topic of her child's sire was forbidden to all. "You did not come this afternoon to discuss my health or the babe. What brought you to my door, Everod? Trouble?"

He and Velouette shared the same aversion for intimacy. Oh, lovemaking was a simple, pleasurable endeavor, one at which they both excelled. What they both avoided went beyond the physical. Neither of them seemed capable of sharing that secret, inner part of their soul. It was obvious to Everod that Solitea shared himself wholly with his duchess. Ramscar, too, seemed at ease with allowing his lady to glimpse those vulnerable aspects of his nature. They were brave men. Everod could not fathom sharing himself, the good and evil, the whole muddled package, with anyone.

Everod had broken their unspoken rule about discussing anything so intimate as her child's sire. Understanding her need to change the subject, he thought it only fair that he distract her with his current troubles.

In truth, he had sought her out for that very reason. She was compassionate, had known sorrow, and above all, Everod thought she might understand in a way Solitea, Cadd, and Ramscar never would.

"Old sins, Vel," he said with a weary sigh. Everod craved a drink stronger than the tea the countess offered, but he refrained from asking for it. "Lord Worrington and his countess have decided to amuse themselves by spending a few months in town."

"Lord Worrington?" Velouette wrinkled her face, attempting to connect the name with her former lover. "I have not heard of him."

"Since his marriage twelve years ago to the former Lady Perton, my father, the Earl of Worrington, has not mingled in polite society," Everod said blandly, waiting for his companion to understand the connection between him and the couple.

"Your father!" she gasped, which turned into a groan when the baby kicked her again. "I did not realize that your father still lived. You never speak of family. I thought you were alone in this world."

Like her. Perhaps that was why they still remained friends, even after they had burned out the passion between them.

"I was fifteen when my father brought his new countess home to Worrington Hall. She was my father's fourth countess, and thirty years younger."

"Merciful heavens! You are like your father, no?" she teased, astounded at the number of wives his sire had buried.

"Not in the slightest," he said through clenched teeth. Everod swiftly leashed his temper. It was not Velouette's fault that he disliked discussing his family. He was the one who had chosen to tell her his one unpardonable sin against his father.

"You must promise me that you will not repeat the tale I am about to tell you. No one knows except the participants, so if I hear—"

"Everod," she said curtly, overriding his threat. "We know each other better than that."

Comforted by her waspish retort, he settled back as he prepared to tell his tale. "My stepmother was beautiful. She would have been slightly younger than you are now. I was fifteen. Innocent . . ." He took a deep breath.

Velouette shook her finger at him. "Liar. I doubt there was a time that anyone could accuse you of innocence!"

Everod snickered at her wry remark. "As innocent as a fifteen-year-old male can be," he amended, and then his expression grew somber. "It was more than beauty that drew me to her. She was vivacious, and a bit naughty. The woman flirted outrageously with everyone and my father seemed to love the attention his new wife received."

"You fell in love with her," Velouette said flatly. "No, wait. I do not mean to mock or criticize your actions. Lest you forget, I met and married my Lord Spryng when I was sixteen."

Everod nodded, ignoring the knot in his throat. "She seemed to encourage my interest. Georgette flirted with me at each encounter. When we were alone, she found reasons to touch me. Each day I became more ensnared by her sensual spell, and before long, it no longer mattered that the lady was my father's wife. I wanted her. No, craved her as I had no other female."

The young countess had taken countless lovers since she had lost her husband to lung fever. She did not blush or shy away from lust. Like him, she embraced it. "Poor Everod. You never stood a chance against this woman, your father's wife, did you?"

Georgette had been his first lover.

Everod did not have to speak his admission aloud. Velouette had already guessed the confusion and shame of his feelings for his stepmother. "Georgette teased me until I was half mad with lust." He shook his head. "I must have been; mad, that is, to have agreed to the chance that we took."

Velouette clenched her fingers into fists. "Georgette was twice married, and nine years older than you," she said tersely. "She knew wholly the risks that she took."

He warmed at her defense. "I wish I had had the

sense to understand that I was being manipulated. But, I was fifteen. Halfway in love with a lady forbidden to me. Even if someone had warned me off, I don't know if I would have refused what she offered."

Everod occasionally summoned that afternoon in his dreams. After weeks of feverish kisses, and letting him clumsily fumble her breasts and skirts, Georgette had offered her body to him. They had slipped away into the back gardens, while his father was conducting business in his library. Neither one had expected him to finish until early evening. Perhaps it was because Georgette had been his first lover that he remembered the details of their brief passionate encounter. He recalled how her blond locks glistened in the sunlight as he pushed her into the tall grass. How her exposed breasts smelled like the flowers around them, and the feel of her feminine flesh as he pushed his cock inside her wet channel.

The memory of Georgette lying beneath him only reminded him of what a fool he had once been. "We had thought no one had noticed that we left the house together. I was supposed to be at the stables, and Georgette had told my father that she was looking over the household accounts."

"Your father saw you?"

Everod smirked as he thought about Maura. Of the miserable girl who choked silently on her tears. "No. Georgette's ten-year-old niece followed us into the gardens. She immediately ran to my father with the news of what she had seen."

Velouette closed her eyes in sympathy. "Mi Dios!" she whispered like a prayer.

"God has little to do with the devil's mischief, Vel," he said dryly, trying to make light of the tragic events that unfolded next. "When I heard my father scream my name, I saw Georgette's beautiful face change from pleasure to a cunning that I did not understand at the time. Maura was screaming and—"

"Maura?"

"Georgette's niece," he said dismissively. "Before I could untangle myself from Georgette's limbs, I felt the sharp edge of my father's blade cut into my throat."

"That awful scar on your throat!"

Tears instantly filled Velouette's eyes, and tumbled down her cheeks. Everod was aghast. He had never seen the woman cry. Ever. He fumbled for his handkerchief and leaned over to press it into her hand. "Vel, there is no need to cry. I know the scar is ugly. Nevertheless, as you can see, I survived my father's attack."

He watched her sniff and dab at her eyes. The actions did little to stem her tears.

"Did your father give you a chance to explain?"

Everod gave her a wary glance when she hiccupped. "What was there to explain? My father had caught his heir tupping his new bride in the back gardens. He did not need a confession."

Only ten-year-old Maura to show him the way.

Velouette tilted her head to the side inquiringly. She sensed there was more to the tale. "What did Georgette tell her husband?"

"While I clutched my throat to keep my life's blood from watering the entire garden, my traitorous stepmother was sobbing and begging her husband's forgiveness for not being strong enough to prevent me from violating her," he said bitterly.

If it was possible to return to that afternoon in the gardens, Everod would have picked up the discarded knife and happily cut Georgette's throat. Unlike his father, he would have succeeded in giving the lady a mortal wound.

"What did you do?"

Agitated, Everod pushed his hand through his hair. The length of it fell an inch past his shoulders. The heavy dark hair helped to conceal his scar from curious lovers.

"I tried not to die," he quipped, using humor to distance himself from the old pain. "A surgeon was summoned. I suppose my father realized belatedly that he might be tried for murder if I had the misfortune to die from his brutal attack. Those first days I was practically mute and out of my mind with fever. I must give Georgette credit for her cleverness. While I lay helpless in my bed, the lady fueled my father's hatred by claiming that she feared a child would result from our unholy union."

"And the niece?"

"She supported her aunt's accusations. Maura told my father that she heard Georgette begging me to stop." He scratched his right brow, recalling that Georgette had been begging, indeed, and it had had nothing to do with him stopping. Everod refrained from mentioning that fact.

Velouette brought her hand to her lips as if she were ill. "Was it true? Was Georgette carrying your child?"

"It was utter nonsense," he snapped. "I had not—there had not been time for me to—" He tried one more time to string the words together. "The faithless bitch lied!"

It was no small effort on Velouette's part, but she rolled out of her chair. Waddling to his side, she embraced him. There was nothing carnal in her actions. In fact, with her breasts and large belly pressing into his side, she felt soft and motherly. Everod patted her on the arm.

"Is this why you do not mention your family? You were banished?"

"Yes." The word escaped his lips as a hiss. "I haven't spoken to my father or younger brother since I was cast out of Worrington Hall."

"This is terrible." She pulled away from him, shaking her head. "Why did you not tell your father the truth? You could have written him a letter detailing your account or sent an emissary?"

He had entertained the same thoughts in the immediate years after his ignoble departure. Anger and pride had held his tongue. It still stung that his father had been so enamored with his wife of six months that he did not even question his son and heir. Worrington had aligned himself and bedded Everod's enemy, and for that, he could never forgive his sire.

"The truth no longer matters, Vel."

Since she was standing close to him, he affectionately placed his hand on her belly. In return, she lightly touched his cheek.

"Worrington and his wife are here in London. If the truth does not matter to you, what does?" Velouette asked, though she saw the answer in his narrowing gaze.

"Revenge."

CHAPTER 6

M aura was certain that Lord Everod was insane.
He had been sending her gifts for the past four
days. Her aunt and uncle were amused that Maura's
few outings had garnered such a shy, ardent admirer.
The earl had believed that his son Rowan had been
sending her the gifts until Rowan had flatly denied the
accusation and likened the gifts to romantic pander.

The first day, Everod had sent her Mrs. Radcliffe's
tomes. The second morning, a gold oval cameo brooch
arrived. In the center was a dove with several flowers
clutched in its beak. Forget-me-nots. On the third day a
delicate bottle of scent arrived. It reminded Maura of a
summer garden.

And finally, on the fourth day, another gift arrived.
Displayed on blue velvet was a silver page turner. The
hand was the figure of a beautiful woman in Grecian
costume. Although entwined wings formed the blade,
all Maura could think of when she glanced down at it
was the bloodied knife Lord Worrington had thrown
to the ground after he had cut Everod's throat. She
could barely bring herself to touch it.

Her aunt and uncle were oblivious to her distress
after each delivery. After excusing herself from the

breakfast room, Maura had calmly climbed the staircase up to her bedchamber, locked the door, and cried until all that was left was hoarse sobs.

Each gift was a message. A taunt to provoke her into action. It was precisely what course of action he was silently directing her to that cost her sleep at night.

By the evening of the fourth day, Maura had come to a decision. Bribing one of the maids, she had a note delivered to Lord Everod's town house. This madness had started at the bookseller's. With luck, she hoped to end it there. She would draw the scoundrel out and confront him. If she was his enemy, then he would have to make his declaration in her presence. Maura could not bear to contemplate what he might send on the fifth day.

This meeting was on her terms. She deliberately arrived earlier than the appointed time so she could watch for his arrival. He would not take her by surprise. Maura felt a flutter of excitement, when at her appointed time of two o'clock, Lord Everod strolled through the front door of the bookseller's. He was so breathtakingly handsome, she might have smiled in greeting, had she not caught herself. This was not the reunion of old friends.

Their meeting this afternoon would define what they might *become*.

"Good afternoon, Lord Everod," Maura said as she curtsied. "My old governess bestowed upon me an appreciation for promptness. To be truthful, I was not certain you would keep our appointment."

His amber eyes with those intriguing green rings glowed with interest as he surveyed her from head to toe. "How could I refuse your gracious offer to renew our old friendship?" he asked, his husky voice carrying far enough for two ladies to glance at her and giggle.

Maura's eyes flared at his insinuation that they were on intimate terms. "We are not—I did no such thing!" she whispered with a fierceness that left her almost breathless. "I—I . . ." She glanced around, already regretting that she had summoned the viscount to the shop. The public place had seemed fitting, safer for their discourse until he had demonstrated that he was willing to risk all, because he had nothing to lose.

She could not make the same boast.

"I thought I could reason with you, but I now see that I have made a grave error asking you here," she said, her misery welling in her eyes.

Everod remained silent, which only increased her agitation and embarrassment.

"May I offer you my compliments, my lord. Your gifts were so clever and cruel. I should have known that I was no match for your wit." She nodded at him. "Good day."

Almost blinded by the tears she fought back, she was unaware that the viscount had followed her out of the bookseller's until he had grabbed her arm. "How dare you? Release me at once! What are you doing?" she demanded as he marched her in the direction of his awaiting carriage.

"Since you find the shop so distasteful, I assumed you would not mind if I offered an alternative," he said, his voice clipped.

He maneuvered her into his carriage with such

admirable ease that Maura wondered how often he dealt with fractious females. "How often do you kidnap ladies off the streets of London?" she asked after he ordered his servant to continue onward.

"Daily," he said humorlessly. Pointedly, he changed the subject. "Since you are here alone, I presume you have been suffering my little gifts in martyred silence. After all what would the family think if they learned that you were the one who demanded that I join you this afternoon?"

His mockery was not worthy of an answer. "How do you know I haven't told your father and Georgette about your mischief?"

"You haven't. I have well-paid eyes and ears in Worrington's household." Everod laughed when her mouth fell open in shock. "I merely jest. It isn't difficult to guess my father's reaction if he believed I was attempting to get my sullied hands on his precious niece. Father would send you and your aunt back to Worrington Hall before either of you could protest."

"I have not told them," she said glumly, confirming his suspicions.

"Tell me something I have not already deduced on my own." He dug into his coat, and retrieved a clean handkerchief. Instead of offering it to her as she had expected, he gently dried the tears on her cheeks. "For instance, where is your coachman? I highly doubt you've been wandering the London streets on your own."

"I told the coachman that there was no reason for him to wait while I shopped. He will return to the bookseller's in two hours. I did not know how much time I would need—" She glanced away, unwilling to finish her admission.

"Poor Maura," Lord Everod said, making a soft sympathetic noise with his tongue. "You haven't challenged too many scoundrels in your young life, have you?"

Her chin lifted at his outrageous statement. "I had no intention of challenging you, my lord. I just wanted to speak with you." Her reasoning sounded weak even to her own ears.

Lord Everod grinned as he folded his handkerchief and tucked it away into a hidden pocket. "How fortuitous! I have desired for the chance to speak with you for a very long time, Maura Keighly," he said so silkily that she almost missed the underlying menace in his tone.

R owan, I am so pleased you were able to pull yourself away from your amusements to visit your family," Georgette said cordially. With her Blenheim spaniel, Beau, filling her arms, she tilted her head and studied the young gentleman she had had a hand in nurturing.

Only three years older than her niece, Rowan Lidsaw was another splendid example of her husband's bloodline. He was tall like his father, and his dark handsome features occasionally sent even her cynical heart racing. Rowan was not an exotic beast like his elder brother, Everod. Everything about him was muted, more conventionable. He was shorter, his build not as broad, nor were his eyes as unique as the banished heir. In spite of this, when Georgette gazed into his pale green eyes, she saw a man who could keep her secrets. A man with whom she could subtly let down her guard, and be more than Worrington's countess.

"Really, Georgette, you speak as if we have not seen each other in months," he chided, circling around her as she closed the door. "I saw you and Father two evenings past."

She turned her cheek upward, expecting a small token of affection.

A dutiful stepson, Rowan leaned closer to brush his lips against her cheek. As soon as he moved in, the white and red chestnut patched spaniel growled threateningly at his intrusion. He abruptly straightened and gave the little dog a baleful look.

"You must forgive Beau, my darling," Georgette said before she murmured soothing unintelligible reassurances to her pet. To Rowan, she said, "My poor baby has not been himself since we left Worrington Hall. Can you believe that he will not eat a single morsel of food unless it comes from my own hand?"

Rowan distanced himself from Georgette and her precious Beau as he sought out a chair in the drawing room. "You spoil that beast, Georgette," he said, not bothering to conceal his disdain. "You have ruined a good animal with your coddling."

Georgette's lips tightened at her stepson's criticism. He had been such an amiable boy when she had married his father. The man he had become could be difficult when he felt slighted. Still, she had learned that there was little distinction when mollifying a man or dog.

"Come, Rowan, do not sulk. I am very pleased to

see you," she said, choosing the sofa adjacent to his chair. Beau laid his head onto her lap, giving her a pleading look with his protruding large liquid dark eyes. The look always managed to twist her heart. She placed her hand on his head, and lightly stroked his long ears.

"Should I ring for some tea?"

"No, thank you. Where is Father?" her stepson demanded, glancing about as if he expected the earl to walk through one of the doors.

"At one of his clubs, I suppose," she said indifferently, not particularly caring where her husband went once he left her side. "I summoned you this afternoon because I felt it was time to discuss your intentions toward my niece."

Exasperated, Rowan curled his left hand around the back of his nape and rubbed his tense muscles. "Damn me! You have made your intentions remarkably clear when you persisted in throwing Maura at me every time I visiting Worrington Hall. Father, on numerous occasions, has reminded me of Maura's intelligence, charm, and beauty." He gave her a steady look. "Fortunately, I happen to agree with you both. I have every intention of marrying your niece. Nevertheless, I am a grown man, Georgette. Let me court Maura in my own manner."

"Your manner is deplorable," she said crisply, not sparing his feelings. "While you spend your evenings at your clubs and bedding your mistress, Maura is being courted by some unknown admirer."

Rowan raised his brows in surprise at her sharp tone. "Father mentioned that Maura has received several gifts. At first, he believed I was the one who was responsible."

"Worrington has already told me that you denied it," she said, disgusted that Rowan had not thought up a clever scheme to court her niece.

Intriguingly, Maura's reaction to her mysterious admirer was a trifle baffling. On that first morning, the books had pleased and flustered her. However, with the arrival of the subsequent gifts, Maura had become quieter, more withdrawn. Oh, she smiled at Worrington and accepted his affectionate teasing good-naturedly, but Georgette understood her niece better than Maura's own parents. Something was troubling the young lady. Did she know the identity of her admirer? If so, for the first time in years, Maura was not confiding in her beloved aunt and that did not bode well.

Discreetly, Georgette had questioned the butler about who was making these deliveries. She had learned that each delivery was made by a different messenger who never offered his name or the name of his employer. This mysterious gentleman was a wrinkle she had not anticipated to her carefully laid plans for Rowan and Maura.

Beau whimpered and rolled onto his back. Too used to satisfying the demands of the men in her life, Georgette obligingly scratched her dog's belly.

Rowan stifled a yawn with his hand. "Have you summoned me to track down Maura's bashful admirer?"

"No," she replied, shaking her head and rolling her eyes upward at his dim-wittedness. "We will deal with this man, if he ever finds the courage to approach my niece. However, there is something that you can do for me."

His lips slowly curled into a grin, and for the first time since he had entered her drawing room, Georgette finally had his attention. "I am yours to command, Lady Worrington."

Oh, how she wished her life were that simple. She gently nudged Beau off her lap, and moved from the sofa to Rowan's side. "Darling boy, you must cease these endless nights of cards and whoring, and concentrate on your future bride. Despite Maura's affection for you, she is not easily won. You must woo her, Rowan. You can be charming when you want to be. Seduce her heart and mind. And if your skills are lacking, then coax her into your bed."

Rowan tipped his head back and laughed. The gesture was so reminiscent of his older brother, Everod, she was momentarily speechless. "Why, Georgette, how vulgar of you to suggest that I should bed Maura to gain her consent to an alliance she obviously does not crave—at least, not as much as you seem to do. What would Father say if he knew of your plans?"

Georgette did not like his shrewd expression. To distract him, she slid onto his lap. "You'll have Worrington's blessing if his grandson already sleeps in Maura's womb." She played idly with a lock of hair near his left ear.

Beau sat up and barked several times. He was jealous of anyone who stole his mistress's attention.

"Infernal dog," Rowan muttered, his gaze focused wholly on Georgette's face. "Its barking will summon a curious servant."

"The staff is used to Beau's barking, and no longer heeds it," she said, gliding her fingers from his hair to his lips. Rowan was feigning indifference; however, his cock had swelled significantly with her bottom pressed against the pliable organ. "Besides, I took the liberty of locking the door. No one will disturb us."

Rowan cleared his throat. "And what do you plan to do with me, Lady Worrington?"

Georgette silenced him with a scorching kiss. Although she was his stepmother, she had never felt motherly toward Worrington's sons. Drawing back, she said huskily, "I will show you how to seduce a lady properly."

Both of them ignored Beau who whined pitifully at his mistress's feet.

For a young lady of two and twenty, Maura was entirely too trusting. This was rather unexpected when one considered the deviousness of her aunt. Everod's limited knowledge of the young woman's life had revealed that she spent months being veritably ignored by her highly intellectual, narcissistic parents only to be sent to Worrington Hall during the summer. His brother, Rowan, timed his visits to the family's country seat when young Miss Keighly was in residence. On the surface, it appeared his younger brother had developed a sweet affection for Georgette's niece.

Staring into her wary sea-gray eyes, he was not completely immune to her vulnerability and artless beauty. Still, Everod did not trust her. "Did you not like my gifts, Maura?"

He discarded formality for the sake of keeping his

quarry off balance. As he had guessed, she blinked at his gentle tone before she looked away.

"Gifts?" She spoke the word so softly that he had to lean closer to hear her. "Is that what you called them when you ordered your man to deliver them to your father's town house?"

His decision to purchase the tomes Maura had been admiring had not been a whim. He sensed that if he had not startled her that afternoon, she would have trotted back to her aunt with her prized books clutched in her hands. It gave him a perverse sense of pleasure knowing that whenever she read Mrs. Radcliffe's tale, she would think of him.

He shrugged. "How did you view them?"

"Warnings," Maura said, hugging herself as if there were a chill in the air. "A taunt; daring me to tell Lord Worrington that you had not forgotten or forgiven any of us."

The young lady beside him was very perceptive. The gifts he had selected were chosen to rattle her composure, and perhaps, send her running from the safety of his father's house. His plan had worked perfectly. After all, instead of sitting in the garden with her nose buried in a book, Maura Keighly had rushed straight to him.

"I presume you did not tell my father of our meeting?" His question was merely a formality. Everod knew she had not.

Maura made a disgruntled sound. "No. The earl thinks I have a mysterious admirer."

Everod tipped his head back and laughed aloud. "A love-smitten beau for Miss Keighly! How rich!"

She blushed a vivid pink hue. "Oh, you think me so plain that no gentleman would have me?" she demanded, her voice rising with her agitation.

He had pricked her feminine pride. A lady in a high temper was unpredictable at best. Everod noted that even his coachman was shaking his head at his lord's obvious blunder.

"You have misunderstood me. It was my father's assumption that amused me, Maura. You are a lovely girl," he added, wincing at the banality of his words.

Maura was not appeased. In truth, she was rather pretty when she was on the verge of committing murder. "See here, Lord Everod. I am not a *child*! I outgrew braids and the desire to climb trees in my bare feet many years ago."

Ah, he had wondered if Maura had recalled those first few months when she had joined her newly married aunt at Worrington Hall. She had raced with him and Rowan across the pastures, gorged on wild berries, and cooled her feet in the stream while the brothers had tried to impress her with their fishing skills.

Everod had been the one who had taught her how to climb a tree. Lord and Lady Courtwill had deemed such frivolous antics to be beneath their only child. He had enjoyed sharing his private world with his new "cousin" until he had been caught in Georgette's silken snare of temptation and lust.

"I see you, Maura Keighly," he said quietly, in stark contrast to her bluster and passion. "I no longer see the child that you were. Except . . ." He stroked the underside of her chin. "Here. And your eyes. A hint of innocence is bewitching in a lady. Is it genuine or has Georgette ruined you, too?"

His question extinguished the vulnerability he found so attractive. He was a jaded rake, and there was no place in his world for innocence. Fragile and rarely valued, it was a quality that never lasted. Everod allowed his hand to fall away from her face.

Maura cleared her throat. "We have drifted from the purpose that has brought us here."

"Your displeasure over my gifts?"

She did not react to his taunt. Instead, she opened her drawstring reticule and slipped her hand into the interior. When she withdrew her hand, her fingers were firmly wrapped around the silver page turner. The point was level with his gut.

Expressionless, Everod eyed the blade. "Are you contemplating murder, Maura?"

The denial flickered in her eyes before she could form a suitable retort to his outrageous question. "I know you must hate me, but how could you possibly believe that I would—"

"Hate you?" he echoed, his brows lifted as he mentally weighed her accusation. "Why would I dwell on hate when there are more appealing passions to explore with a beautiful lady?"

Her lips formed a soundless O. Recalling her task, she presented the page turner to him point down. Once he had accepted her offering, she continued to dig in her reticule. A moment later, the scent bottle was laid carefully on top of the page turner. Before he could protest, she had retrieved the cameo brooch. "Forgive me for not bringing Mrs. Radcliffe's tomes.

They would not fit in my reticule, and I did not want anyone—"

"Maura."

From her expression and the stiffness of her posture, she had prepared a speech for him in advance. Switching the glass scent bottle to his other hand, he tucked the silver page turner in one of the inner pockets of his frock coat. At a loss for what to do with the scent bottle, he wrapped it in his handkerchief and it also disappeared within the confines of his coat. He sat back and decided to hear her out.

"I want to compliment you on your fine taste, my lord. The gifts you selected were innocuous to the casual observer, and yet each one had the desired reaction you anticipated," she said, pausing as she drew in a ragged breath. The tears he had thought banished filled her eyes, heightening her air of misery.

Everod shifted uncomfortably on the bench. "Maura."

She held up a hand. "Pray, let me finish. I did not reveal to your father or my aunt your calculated approach, because I had deduced that it was exactly what you wanted me to do." Realizing that she was still holding the brooch, she placed in his palm.

"I never had the chance to speak to you after . . ." She gulped more air, making him wonder if she was prone to fainting. "After." Maura could not seem to say the words, and Everod was not going to make it easy for her.

Getting control over her volatile emotions, she continued, "If we had encountered each other the next day, week, or month, I would have told you how much

I regretted my part in your banishment. If I had known your father would have attacked his own son in such a violent manner, I never would have—"

Her hesitant, tearful apology angered him beyond reason. "Have done what, Maura? Followed me and your aunt into the gardens and spied on us, watching me as I pushed Georgette's skirts above her waist and shoved my co—"

"Enough!" she yelled, squeezing her eyes shut as if to block the memory of that afternoon.

Everod almost reached for her. She looked so fragile and partially broken when he had yet to begin the torment he had planned for her.

Before he could move, Maura opened her eyes. "I am not asking for your forgiveness for my part that day. It would be a fruitless exercise, because I do not think you are capable of it."

He smiled at her insult. "Maura, my sweet, you will have to do better to puncture my composure. Kittens have sharper claws than you."

Maura tugged on the strings of her reticule. "I have no intention of challenging you, my lord. You are harder, crueler, and stronger than I could ever hope to become."

"Why, thank you, m'dear!"

"I did not mean it as a compliment," she snapped, some of her earlier bravado returning. "You delivered a message to me, and I decided to return the favor."

"And what message would that be, Maura?"

"Find another pawn, Lord Everod. Twelve years ago, I was an unwilling player in a deep game of intrigue I was too young to comprehend. My ignorance cost you your family, and I have to live with that fact for the rest of my life."

"You're getting awfully close to that apology you vowed never to offer," he teased.

"Coachman, stop the carriage!" she ordered harshly, reminding him nauseatingly of her aunt.

He calmly told the servant to ignore her command.

Furious at being outmaneuvered, she yelled, "And you, Lord Everod can go straight to perdition!

"Insults will not provoke me into dumping your sweet arse onto the filthy streets without a protector, even if you do deserve it," he said, his indulgence toward her temper waning.

"This was a pointless endeavor," she muttered. "I want to return to the bookseller's shop."

Everod nodded to the coachman. "You heard Miss Keighly, Sam. Turn us about."

Their self-imposed silence was not broken until the coachman shouted for the team to halt. The moment it was safe to do so, Maura climbed over Everod's legs, intending to descend the carriage without anyone's assistance.

"Ho!" Everod said, catching Maura by the waist and steadying her before she tumbled headfirst out of the carriage. "Everyone watching your hasty escape from my carriage will think I plucked your virtue in front of all and sundry."

"As one of the most notorious members of *les sauvages nobles,* you have most certainly refused few dares," Maura said tightly. "Now let me go."

So the gossips had already filled her head with cautionary tales about him and his friends. Or had

Georgette been telling lies about him to keep her niece away from Worrington's evil, lecherous heir? Her derision set off his temper faster than a bolt of lightning.

"Indeed, it is a fine day for a walk," the coachman cheerfully remarked to no one in particular. Extremely diligent in protecting Lord Everod's privacy, he had noticed that the arguing couple had drawn a few curious spectators. He offered the pedestrians a benign smile as he waited for Miss Keighly to descend. The servant was confident his lord would not detain the lady in front of witnesses.

Everod grabbed her elbow, before she could escape. He jerked her closer so his lips brushed her ear. "The tales you've heard about me are only the ones that can be told in polite company. Trust me, I have done worse. I'm a scoundrel, a notorious rake, Maura, and you have whetted my base appetites. Run, little girl. I love a good chase."

Shaken, Maura gladly accepted his coachman's hand, and descended the carriage. She headed for the open doorway of the bookseller's shop. To his disappointment, she did not glance back.

CHAPTER 7

"I hear you have taken to terrorizing young virgins on the streets," Xavier, the proprietor of Moirai's Lust said to Everod later that evening when he and Cadd had eschewed an evening of crowded ballrooms and tepid lemonade for the civility of the gambling hell.

"Vile rumors," he replied, eyeing his cards. "I prefer wilder prey."

Cadd gestured for the blond giant who had the build of a blacksmith to join them, but the man politely refused with quick shake of his head.

"Speaking of untamed, where is your delightful partner this evening?" Everod asked, thinking of his past encounters with the flirtatious but unattainable brunette who helped Xavier turn a well-deserved profit. If his luck with cards this evening was any indication, he would not be retiring to his bed alone.

"Out of reach," the proprietor said, bracing his fist on the table. It was impossible to miss the ripple of muscle as he stretched the seams of his elegant black coat. "Go apologize to your virgin, Everod."

His warning delivered, Xavier lifted his head and caught sight of a quarrel brewing across the room. On a muttered oath, he charged across the room prepared to use his fists if his noble patrons could not behave in his establishment.

"I would reconsider," Cadd said, his attention no longer on the cards.

"Reconsider what?" Everod tossed his cards face-down in disgust and reached for the bottle of wine between them.

Cadd gathered up both their cards. "Fighting Xavier."

"You do not think it would be a fair match?" Quietly, Everod simmered. What a fine friend Cadd was to assume Everod could not crack that blond giant's head!

"Physically I think you are a good match. However, he has something in his favor that you do not." Cadd gestured at the cards, but Everod was not in the mood to play anymore.

"And what is that?"

The marquess set aside the cards, and clasped his hands together. "Xavier views Moirai as his, even if she refuses to acknowledge his claim. That man will kill anyone foolish enough to touch her. Besides, you are not really interested in her."

Feeling peevish, Everod glared at his friend. "Who says I'm not?"

"I do." Cadd took the bottle from Everod and re-filled his own glass. "If you were interested in tumbling Xavier's woman, you would have done so months ago. I recognize that look in your eye." He shook his finger knowingly at him. "You want a fight more than a woman."

"Shut your bone box!" Everod sneered, refusing to

admit that Cadd had understood what his friend had
wanted better than he had all evening. "You must be
already foxed to be spouting such nonsense."

"Who is the virgin?" At Everod's sudden stillness,
Cadd made a placating gesture with his hands. "I assume there is a woman. Xavier's sources are usually
quite accurate."

"Maura—Miss Maura Keighly," Everod said, scrub-
bing his face. His exchange with the prickly young
woman had plagued him the rest of the afternoon until he had sought out his friend. "She is Lady Worrington's niece, and is presently residing at their town
house."

The marquess whistled soundlessly at his revelation. "What haven't you told me?"

Everod shrugged dispassionately. "She was part of
what happened twelve years ago."

Cadd seized Everod's wrist before he could touch
his glass. "Look. You have never been one to back
away from a fight. However, as one of your closest
friends, I am asking you to stay away from the Worringtons and Miss Keighly."

The solemn request was so uncharacteristic of the
marquess that Everod was speechless. They had spent
years taunting each other into wagers that might have
cost them their lives. They had acted as each other's
seconds in duels, and fought side by side in tavern
brawls. Cadd was the last person he expected to tell
him to back away from a fight. Laughing, he shook
off the man's hold on his wrist. "You jest."

"Actually, I'm not. Unless you are prepared to apologize to your father—"

"I'm not."

"Then I see no reason for you to provoke a confrontation," Cadd said in such a reasonable tone that Everod was tempted to punch him for it. "And what of Miss Keighly?"

"She is no one's business but my own."

"Now you sound like Xavier. She must have been a child twelve years ago."

"Is there a point to this lecture?"

"My point is, Miss Keighly is not responsible for you getting your throat cut twelve years ago. You did that very nicely on your own when you fucked your father's wife," Cadd said bluntly.

"Christ, Cadd! Lower your voice," Everod hissed. "Why not spare your voice and post it in the papers."

"I understand your pain, my friend. You crave revenge for Lady Worrington's treachery, and she has been unattainable. The niece, however, is another matter. Are you any better than your stepmother if you take your revenge on an innocent young woman?"

Everod had heard enough. Rising, he leaned against the edge of the table as he stared down at his friend. Cadd held Everod's gaze, refusing to back down. "We all lost our innocence that afternoon, Cadd. Stay out of my way when it comes to my family and Miss Keighly. I'm not selective these days about who is feeling the impact of my fist or facing the wrong end of my pistol."

You wanted to see me, Aunt Georgette?" Maura asked, lingering at the threshold of her uncle's library.

Georgette was watching the jobbers as they maintained the immaculate gardens below. Her rigid posture and her hands fisted at her sides revealed that Maura's futile attempt not to be drawn into her aunt's private war with her stepson had failed. Someone had been whispering in Georgette's ear.

"Yesterday, you never mentioned seeing Everod."

Her aunt had yet to turn around and greet her. The absence of warmth and recognition hinted at the depth of her ire. Maura stepped into the large room and shut the door.

"What did you hear?"

Georgette slowly faced her. Adorned in white and her light blond hair piled artfully on top of her head, her aunt looked like a vengeful goddess. "More to the point, dearest niece, why did I not hear the news about my notorious stepson from *you*?"

Shame heated Maura's cheeks for her deliberate omission. Guilt, duty, and loyalty swirled in her stomach until it bubbled up into her throat and choked her. "It is not a secret that Lord Everod spends much of his time in London. You and Uncle both knew this, and still you chose to travel to town for the social season. Did you really believe you could mingle with the *ton*, among his friends, and not encounter him? A confrontation was inevitable."

"I am not a fool, Maura," her aunt said, seething. "Of course a confrontation was inevitable. Everod is not a coward. However, any contact was to occur on *my* terms! I was to choose the manner and the setting. *Me!* Not some silly fumbling twit of a girl who likely piddled on her petticoats the moment he approached her!"

Was that how Georgette saw her?

Her aunt's rage and barbed insults stung Maura like an unexpected ice storm. Wrapping her arms in a comforting gesture, she tried to make the older woman see reason. "No harm was done, Aunt. It was a simple, brief conversation—"

Georgette struck Maura across the face.

"Do not *ever* try to lie to me again!" Her eyes were narrow slits as she pointed an accusing finger at her niece. "There were witnesses, Maura. You were seen scrambling out of his carriage like a frightened grouse. That means you spoke to him at the shop, long enough for him to coax you into his carriage where a more private discourse occurred away from prying eyes. If you possess the intelligence your parents are always claiming, then you will repeat your conversation with him word for word."

Maura staggered backward. No one, not even her parents, had ever laid an abusive hand on her. Horrified, she covered her throbbing cheek with her trembling hand. There was only one other incident that had provoked her aunt to hurt her. It was the day Maura was forced to tell Lord Worrington that his elder son had violated his new stepmother.

"You try my patience, Maura."

With hurt gleaming like moonlight, Maura turned away. She needed distance from her aunt; time to choose her words carefully. "Did you consider that I might have been attempting to protect you, Aunt? After all, you claimed twelve years ago that Lord Everod attacked you. Since that day, his name has never been uttered in my presence. Is it so outlandish to believe that I would not want to upset you again by reminding you of the terrifying incident?"

Maura collapsed onto the sofa, refusing to glance at her aunt. All the reasons she offered were valid, but the immense chasm of her omissions distanced her from her aunt.

Contrite, Georgette glided to Maura's side. She sat gingerly beside her. "Forgive me. I have been so over-wrought by the thought of seeing Everod again that I did not fully appreciate your actions. All I saw were lies and betrayal. Naturally, you would want to pro-tect me."

Maura turned her head and faced Georgette. She swallowed, trying to ease the dryness in her throat. The apology was given not only in words, it was there in her aunt's sorrowful expression. The sting from Geor-gette's slap was too fresh for Maura to forgive. Lady Worrington could wring emotion as skillfully as any stage player.

Her aunt opened her arms. More out of habit, Maura accepted her embrace. "Oh, my poor girl, my treasured one," Georgette crooned into Maura's hair. "You must have been so frightened when Everod cornered you. Alone. No one to protect you." She pulled back to see her niece's face. "Did he hurt you?"

"No, Aunt." *Unlike you.* "As you said, there were witnesses to our encounter," Maura said woodenly. "Lord Everod inquired about the family, and asked that I pass along his respects. Considering the awk-ward situation, I thought it best not to upset either you or Uncle."

Maura stared down at her clasped hands resting on

her lap. She mentally willed her aunt to believe her. When she told Everod that she refused to be anyone's pawn again, she had been truthful.

After a moment of silence, Georgette nodded and smoothed a strand of Maura's face that had been glued to her face by her tears. "Of course. You thought only of your family. You are a good girl, Maura. My accusations were wholly unfounded. I found myself regretting my hurtful words even as I uttered them."

"May I be dismissed?" Maura said, cringing at her subservient soft tone.

"Yes. Go wash your face and rest. We are attending the theater this evening, and I want you looking your best for Rowan," Georgette said soothingly, her expression revealing that her thoughts had jumped to her grand plans for her niece.

Maura slipped out of her aunt's embrace. She remained silent as she stood and walked stiffly to the door.

"Maura?"

She halted with her hand on the latch, her back to her aunt.

"You were correct in wanting to protect Worrington. He would be very distressed to learn that Everod had approached you."

Maura looked askance when her aunt seemed to hesitate. "If Everod tries to speak with you again, I think it best for your own good that you tell me immediately. For now, I see no reason to let Worrington know that his heir is not above using you to hurt me again." Georgette gave her a tremulous smile. "I could not bear it if Everod hurt you, my treasure."

"Nor I, Aunt Georgette."

Maura quietly closed the door.

Patience Knowden, Countess of Ramscar, had been promised by her husband a thrilling evening at the theater. He should have warned her that most of the drama would take place in the boxes instead of the stage below. First, Ram disappeared through the drawn box curtains with Cadd, Mr. Brawley or Mac as he preferred to be called by his friends, and Solitea regarding business with *les sauvages nobles*.

This was not the first evening she had sat next to an empty chair while Ram settled disagreements between his male friends. Resigned, she was prepared to enjoy the play alone. However, once the gentlemen had departed, Solitea's duchess, Kilby, and his sister, Fayre, began a heated whispered exchange. Someone had caught the ladies' attention in one of the private boxes to the right.

Unable to resist the developing intrigue, Patience slid into her husband's chair. "I surrender. What has happened? Is it dangerous? Has someone issued a challenge?"

Although Ram refused to discuss the subject of dueling, Patience had not forgotten that he had once challenged a gentleman on her behalf. The other man had cried off, and his seconds had conveyed his apologies. It had been a dreadful ordeal. Ram's father had died from mortal wounds he had sustained in a duel. She would not lose her husband in the same manner.

Fayre, Maccus Brawley's wife, noticed her concern and clasped her hand in sympathy. She had been born a Carlisle. The poor woman had been surrounded by obstinate, reckless males her entire life.

"No one has been challenged," Fayre assured her, her green eyes sparkling with compassion. "Not yet, anyway."

Relieved, Patience closed her eyes. "Which one is in trouble?"

Kilby leaned closer so no one could overhear their conversation. "Everod," she replied, her expression not as composed as her sister-in-law's.

"Everod?" Patience blinked in surprise at the revelation. "He has yet to arrive. I realize the viscount can be rather maddening, but a challenge preceding his arrival surpasses my expectations of the gentleman." She squinted in the general direction that had caught her friends' interest, but she noted nothing extraordinary about the occupants.

"I suppose this involves a lady."

It had not taken long in Everod's company for Patience to deduce that the viscount was an unapologetic scoundrel. There was no denying he had a certain charm about him that might tempt a lady to risk her reputation for the chance of winning his heart. She would never admit it to a soul, especially not her husband, but even she had not been immune to Everod's beguiling smile and silent invitation to be wicked with him.

Patience sighed. Both ladies glanced questioningly at her. "Well, there always seems to be a lady involved when we discuss Everod," she said defensively.

"Not precisely," Kilby whispered, discreetly concealing her hand as she pointed to the right. "The gentleman. Eight boxes across from us. Does he seem familiar to you?"

Before she had married Ramscar, Patience had traveled the countryside as an unremarkable player in rural theaters and fairs. She had been a rather competent petty thief, though it was not a profession she had been proud of, or one she boasted of to the *ton*. Nevertheless, the skills she had learned served her well in polite society.

Opening her fan with a flourish, she stirred the warm air as she discreetly sought out the gentleman that had caught Kilby's and Fayre's attention. She found him easily as she feigned boredom, allowing her eyes to focus on the box next to her quarry. It took a moment for her peripheral vision to gather the details she needed. He was an older gentleman. Over sixty. His hair had silvered and thinned, but he had a full head which was clipped close to his scalp. Although he was seated, she could deduce he was tall and obviously well fed if his slight paunch was any indication. It was difficult to tell from this angle, but from her point of view, he was a good-looking gentleman. There was a certain solicitous charm about him as he chatted quietly with his lady.

A certain charm . . .

Patience suddenly felt dizzy. "Good grief, is he—"

Fayre nodded, the diamond in her cinnamon tresses glittering in the dim lamplight. "Everod's father, Lord Worrington. The lady next to him is his fourth Lady Worrington."

Patience risked a second, more direct look at the blond woman. "Are you certain? She seems young enough to be his daughter." She hastily stared down at her lap. "No, you are correct. She is not his daughter."

Kilby giggled. "Not when she has her hand on his—"

"Kilby!" Fayre hushed her sister-in-law.

"Well, there are dark corners aplenty in this place," the duchess said, enjoying herself. "Such a public display is an invitation for idle speculation."

All three ladies giggled, then quickly sobered when a gentleman from another box cleared his throat.

"Who is the other lady sitting beside Lady Worrington?" Patience asked her companions. "Everod's sister?"

"My sister? Heaven forbid," Everod whispered behind them, startling all three ladies. "All the same, I suspect Lord and Lady Worrington will not be overjoyed when they learn of my plans for Miss Maura Keighly."

There was a noticeable chill to the air as the viscount glared at his family. Patience turned away, resisting the urge to rub her bare arms. She noticed a young gentleman had joined the Worringtons. Everod swore. Without a word, he straightened and left the box.

It was only then that Patience noticed her husband, Mac, and Solitea. She stood and walked around the empty chairs to greet them. "Who is he?" she asked Ram.

He had already told her that the viscount had been cast from his own family years ago. Everod had not struck her as someone who was embittered about his past. The gentleman who had stormed out of the box, however, seemed capable of murder.

"Mr. Rowan Lidsaw," her husband replied, signaling for Cadd and Solitea to follow their angry friend. "Everod's younger brother."

Both gentlemen seemed troubled and that heightened Patience's concern. Mac walked toward the seated ladies, and sat beside his wife. Fayre murmured something to her husband, who replied, but the orchestra playing below and the buzz of conversation from the other boxes prevented her from eavesdropping. Mac placed his arm around Fayre and kissed her reassuringly on the temple.

Patience stared up at her husband. She sensed his urgency, his need to leave her once again and join his friends as they rushed to Everod's defense. "Ram, what is happening?"

"Uninvited family," he replied as he lifted the curtain to leave.

Hesitating, he released the curtain and pulled her close to him. Ram lowered his head and kissed her, lingering over the task until she was breathless.

"Family?" she echoed, swaying in his arms.

There was a hint of regret in his gaze as he released

her and pushed the curtain aside. "You know better than all of us that some families can never be mended. That some betrayals are too painful for simple words to heal."

CHAPTER 8

After her altercation with her aunt, Maura had prepared for their evening together. Her demeanor was subdued. Her uncle had commented on her melancholy, noting that her cheeks were flushed with color. He worried that she was ill, but Georgette assured him that what he perceived as illness was simply a case of nerves.

"At least pretend to be grateful for your generous circumstances," her aunt hissed in her ear, when Worrington was distracted by another gentleman as they entered the lobby of the theater.

Aunt Georgette's warning was clear. Maura was to behave and not call attention to herself, or she would be returning to Worrington Hall alone. Unfortunately, her aunt's threat did not instill the fear she had hoped in her sullen niece.

Lost in thought, Maura fingered the pearl and silver necklace Georgette had given her before their journey. The polished silver gleamed against her skin. In spite of her resentment toward her aunt, she treasured the gift. The necklace was too mundane to be appreciated by the present Lady Worrington. According to her aunt, if it did not glitter or cost a small fortune, it was not worthy of her body.

Her arrival at the theater did little to improve her mood. The box her uncle had procured was chosen for its advantageous view of the other boxes. The view and the enjoyment of the theatrics on the stage below was a secondary concern. She listened to the orchestra, but the only voices that could be heard above the din of the audience were those of the patrons sitting in the adjacent boxes.

"Rowan, how good of you to join us this evening," her aunt gushed, extending her hand out regally so he could admire the new emerald and diamond ring Worrington had bought her.

"My lady," Rowan said, bowing over her hand. "Father."

Maura tensed when his blue eyes rested on her face.

"Miss Keighly, I vow you grow more enchanting in my absence," he said, bowing.

"Then pray leave me, sir," Maura said, retrieving her hand when he seemed reluctant to release her. "Perhaps at our next meeting, I will be worthy of a higher compliment."

The earl chortled at his niece's wit.

Sweetly smiling at him, Maura said, "What say you, Uncle? Should I strive for fascinating or beguiling?"

"If another opinion is welcome," Everod said, parting the curtains, "I would choose the word *tempting* to describe you, Miss Keighly. Though *luscious* also suits you, I am certain my father would view the word a trifle bold."

Everod.

Maura felt her heartbeat quicken at his unexpected appearance. Leave it to the viscount to foil Georgette's carefully laid plans and pick his own moment to acknowledge the family who had banished him.

The Lidsaws seemed frozen, uncertain how to respond. They were in a public place, after all. Maura had the sudden urge to laugh.

Everod must have sensed her amusement because the heat of his amber-green gaze touched her face. His interest drifted lower to the soft swell of her breasts.

How rude!

Expecting a mocking comment, Maura was puzzled when his gaze shot back up to meet her eyes. She could not understand the anger that had flashed, replacing his high-handed humor.

The viscount recovered swiftly. His stance wide, and his hands clasped behind his back, Everod stared down at his family. "Have you no words of welcome for your heir, Father? What about you, sweet stepmother?" He sighed as if disappointed. "Come now, Rowan. You have not seen your elder brother in twelve years. Is that not worth a brotherly embrace?"

Lord Worrington was the first to recover. Her aunt Georgette looked properly tragic as she grasped her husband's forearm to silently remind him that half of the theater's patrons were most likely witnessing their exchange.

"You are not welcome here," the earl said, the words sounding as if they had been torn from his throat, leaving him bleeding and raw.

Maura shifted slightly and noticed that Everod had not come alone. Beyond the curtain, the shadowy figures of two or three men waited silently for the viscount to deliver his message to the Lidsaws.

And her.

She could not forget that he viewed her as the enemy, too.

"Are you deaf, Brother?" Rowan said, his tone so icy, Maura had thought the younger sibling incapable of it. "You have caused our family enough pain. If you feel it necessary, you may try again in another twelve years. Maybe then we will have forgotten your treachery."

Everod's jaw clenched in restrained fury. Taking a stalking step toward his brother, he sneered in contempt when Rowan deliberately placed himself in front of Georgette as if to protect her.

"Treachery?" the viscount said, looking down his nose. To Rowan's credit, he did not flinch. Everod shook his head. "Father married it, you protect it, and I fucked it twelve years ago. I have yet to clean the stench from my nostrils."

Rowan charged him, bumping his chest against Everod, daring him to raise his fist against his brother.

Maura stood, grabbing him by the arm. "Rowan, no!" she said in a harsh whisper, hoping her voice would not carry beyond the private box. They had already gained enough spectators. "Not here."

Everod's friends entered the box. Whether they were prepared to fight with their friend or stop him from attacking his brother had not been determined.

For her interference, the viscount glared at her. "Yes, Brother. By all means, listen to Miss Keighly.

After all, the Lidsaw men have a notoriously sad history of allowing their cocks to rule over logic."

"I do not fear you, you smug arrogant bastard!"

Lord Worrington seized Rowan's arms from behind before he could launch himself at his older brother. Everod crossed his arms and laughed at them all.

"Get out of here!" Georgette hissed at him, her composure crumbling as she recognized that her stepson had won this skirmish. "Get out!"

With a final smirk at Maura, the viscount departed with his friends.

I thought it went rather well," Ram said, breaking the tense silence. "No one was punched, no challenges issued, and we have yet to be tossed out of the theater. If our luck holds, my wife will not punish me for abandoning her this evening."

Everod threaded his hands through his hair as he reached one of the dimly lit corridors that connected the boxes and circled around to open up into private saloons and a main staircase. Out of frustration, he slammed his fist into the nearby wall and welcomed the lightning bolt of pain that traveled up his arm.

"Feel better?" Solitea asked, not making the mistake of touching him.

"No!" he replied, his voice an ominous growl. His father had not seen him since he had been cast out, and the old man held nothing in his heart but contempt for him. Georgette had even corrupted his brother. The hatred in Rowan's face clawed at him. "I would have felt better if I had tossed that lying bitch over the balcony."

"Miss Keighly?"

Everod curled his lip at Cadd. Only he would dare to bait him, when he was so close to losing control. "I told you to leave Maura out of this."

He brushed by the marquess, using his shoulder to clear the way. Ramscar shrugged at Solitea. The pair always seemed to be passing silent signals between them, and it was damn irritating at times.

He strode down the hall, uncaring if his friends followed. In fairness, Solitea and Ram had wives to look after. Responsibilities. He could not expect them to turn their backs on their lives just because he was angry and hurting.

Hurting.

The unspoken admission stopped him cold. With his back against the wall, he slid down until he sat on his haunches. It was humiliating to realize that after all these years he was still seeking his father's approval. Or did he want absolution for succumbing to Georgette's wiles?

Solitea crouched down next to him. "What were you hoping to gain from ambushing your family this evening?"

Everod had been standing in one of the upper balconies when he glanced down and saw his father, Georgette, and Maura enter the lobby. Even from his position, he could tell Maura was upset. Georgette had tugged on her niece's elbow harshly and he had realized that all was not well between the pair. Someone had told the older woman that Everod had been sniffing around her innocent niece. Maura had likely suffered for his actions.

"Honestly," he said, holding his friend's unwavering

gaze, "I don't know. Whatever I had hoped to gain, it wasn't there."

What Everod did not admit to his friends were his reasons for approaching the Lidsaws. He knew what had spurred him to enter the Worringtons' private box. It was Rowan. His friends would laugh at his hypocrisy, but he did not like the carnal awareness in his brother's eyes when they settled on Maura. In a sudden flash, he knew his brother intended to bed her. The unpalatable thought sent Everod down the corridor with the intention of breaking his brother in half.

Watching Maura as she tried to soothe and restrain Rowan, the way she touched his brother's arm with familiarity, had ignited his temper, and he had struck out at her, too. She should have been approaching him. It was *his* temper she should crave to appease, not Rowan's.

I must be bloody mad.

Loathing. Pain. Loneliness. Need.

A seething hurricane was swirling inside him, and at the center he saw Maura Keighly staring at him with her wary sea-gray eyes.

Everod wanted something from her. He had too much pride to ask. When he figured out what he wanted, he was likely to just take it from her, uncaring of the price both of them would pay.

In the end, he would hurt her.

It was inevitable.

I s that you, Maura?"

Maura froze. Muted light bathed her face as her uncle opened the library door and stood at the threshold with a branch of candles in his hand. "Uncle, I thought you had retired with Aunt Georgette?"

"I could not sleep," was his tired reply.

Maura sighed. "Neither could I."

She remained silent on the reasons that had sent her scurrying out of her bedchamber, when she longed for the oblivion of sleep.

All three of them.

On her dressing table lay the brooch, the bottle of scent, and the silver page turner she had returned to Everod. She had seen him stuff the items in his frock coat, and yet there they were in her private rooms. It was another message. The man was reminding her he could breach the Worrington walls anytime he wanted to reach her. There was no place she could run and hide from him.

"Step inside, Niece," the earl said gruffly. "I know what cures restlessness."

Maura stepped into the library, noting the room was dark except for the lively flames flickering in the fireplace and the branch of candles in her uncle's hand. She watched as he set the silver candelabra on the low table in front of her, and moved to pour her a glass of what he had been drinking before her interruption.

Pinching the delicate base, Worrington offered her the glass. "Golden cordial," he said, though the coloring of the liqueur had a reddish cast to it. "Created from one of my grandmother's recipes. The old dear was rather clever when it came to potions. Very much like your aunt."

Maura was intimately acquainted with her aunt's medicinal potions. The countess had a midwife's cleverness when it came to creating herbal tinctures that were meant to instill vigor in the weak, cure headaches, or a stomach ail. Throughout her life, Aunt Georgette had insisted on keeping extensive gardens as she honed her skills. There were very few members of the household staff that had not imbibed one of their mistress's concoctions.

She smiled tentatively at the earl. "Thank you, Uncle," Maura said, taking a sip from the glass. It was sweet with a hint of orange flavoring. "It is very good."

The earl acknowledged her compliment with a nod. He froze as something about Maura caught his attention, his smile fading in puzzlement. He peered closely at her. "That necklace. I haven't seen—Where the devil did you get it?"

The man recognized the piece. Maura nervously fingered the ornate silver pendant of beads and set pearls, suddenly aware her aunt had not told Lord Worrington that she had given one of the old family pieces away.

"Aunt Georgette gave it to me. The pearls did not suit her, and she assured me that you would not mind," she explained. Releasing the pendant, she shifted in her seat and leaned forward to set her cordial on the small round table positioned near her chair. "I can give it back to you—"

The earl shackled both wrists to prevent her from removing the necklace. "No, don't bother." He released her when she had complied. Absently, he lifted the pendant and brushed his thumb across the ornate surface.

"It was a surprise to see the piece, you see," her uncle confessed. "No one has worn it in decades. In truth, I had forgotten its existence until I saw it gleaming in the firelight. Did you know, the necklace was part of a suite? There were earrings, a bracelet, and a ring, if I recall. Did Georgette give them to you?"

Maura shifted, uncomfortable that he had yet to release the pendant. "No, Uncle. I doubt Aunt Georgette was aware that there were other pieces. Perhaps they have been lost?"

"Lost. Yes." Worrington did not seem angry that his wife had given away an old trinket. However, he seemed to grow melancholy as he stared at the pendant.

He finally allowed the pendant to slip from his fingers. His movements slow and tired, he hobbled to the sofa where his glass of cordial awaited. In a movement uncharacteristically informal for the earl, he leaned against the cushions and stretched out his long limbs.

Maura quietly sipped her cordial, silently debating if she should pursue the subject of the pendant. It was preferable to discussing Everod's brief, hostile appearance in the private box.

"I have not thanked you properly for the necklace, Uncle," she said, enjoying the warmth the cordial was creating within her. "If I may inquire, who was the original owner of the necklace?"

Worrington did not immediately react to her question. Staring at the fire through his cordial glass, he seemed lost in his private thoughts. Maura was on the verge of repeating the question when he said, "I purchased the jewelry suite for my first countess, Everod's mother. Pearls were her favorite. She loved the simplicity of them, you see."

Maura glanced at the pendant. She stroked the large center pearl as she recalled Everod's expression. Like his father, he had recognized the pendant as belonging to his mother.

Perhaps he thinks I stole it?

She frowned at the unpleasant thought. Everod had seemed so angry this evening. She had noticed how his jaw had tightened when he glanced in her direction, but she had not connected his ire to the pendant Georgette would have melted down if Maura had not taken it.

"Aunt Georgette did not know the history of the necklace when she gave it to me," Maura said, feeling heartsick that she had given Everod another reason to despise her.

Her uncle chuckled. "Georgette cares little about history. The piece is too simple, too old-fashioned for her." He turned his head to face her. "However, the necklace suits you, Niece. Everod's mother would have been pleased to see you wear it, though it might be best if you do not mention to your aunt who the original owner of the necklace was."

Maura concurred. Her aunt was possessive, and preferred to forget that the earl had married three times before he pledged himself to her. "She would not be pleased."

"Indeed."

If Georgette learned that Worrington had bought the necklace for Everod's mother, she might insist that the trinket be destroyed.

CHAPTER 9

Both her aunt and uncle had failed to appear in the breakfast room the next morning. Maura was relieved. She had come to a decision before she had succumbed to Worrington's fine cordial last evening, and if her aunt learned of Maura's plans, the lady would be furious.

She waited until late morning before she took action. It was still much too early for the quality to be out, but this, too, suited Maura. Used to family and servants ignoring her, she told Abbot that she was off to attend a scientific lecture at the British Museum. Her parents were known for their eccentricities. The butler did not consider it odd that their only daughter had developed the same passion for intellectual pursuits.

Once the coachman had delivered her to Great Russell Street, Maura hired a hackney to take her the rest of her journey.

Everod's town house.

It was risky to confront the viscount, especially after the nasty confrontation with his family. However, Maura had no intention of boldly knocking on the gentleman's door and demanding to see Lord Everod.

She planned to remain long enough to deliver the item that was rightfully the viscount's to his manservant, and then she would return to the museum.

No one would ever know she ventured anywhere near the beast's lair.

E verod was dressing for a morning ride, when he heard his manservant open the front door. Curious about his morning caller, he donned his coat and headed for the stairs.

"Who was it?" Everod called down as he watched his man, Dunley, close the door.

"A delivery, my lord."

He stifled an unexpected surge of disappointment. "I hope you set the gent straight that all deliveries are made in the back."

"Aye, m'lord. This one was of a personal nature." Dunley held up a small leather case. "The coachman said the lady would not leave her card. However, she insisted that you would understand."

Maura.

"Order the driver to halt!" Everod shouted, and the manservant turned to carry out his lord's command.

So Maura had come to him. He rushed down the stairs and leaped the last four steps. It had taken several well-placed bribes to return his gifts while the Worringtons were out for the evening. After the angry exchange at the theater, he marveled at the young lady's courage.

Dunley had succeeded in stopping the coach not far from his residence. The two men were arguing, and Everod could hear Maura's soft voice as she pleaded for the coachman to drive on.

Everod opened the door of the coach. Maura groaned when she saw him. "Good morning, Miss Keighly," he said, slightly out of breath. "A bit early for calls, is it not?"

Vexed, Maura glared at him. "I am not calling on you, Lord Everod. I did not even leave a card! If you will call off your man, I will be on my way."

"Dunley, give me the case," he ordered the manservant. He grinned at Maura. "Since you are here, you might as well come in. Cook will make you some tea."

"No, thank you." She bit out each word. "I have other plans. Besides, it would be unseemly."

"Not really, miss," Dunley cheerfully interjected. "His lordship is having ladies at all hours."

"That will be enough, Dunley." Everod silenced the manservant with a narrowed glance. Maura was already skittish of him. If there had been any chance of convincing her to sit in his drawing room, Dunley had ruined it with his loose tongue.

"I never intended to stay, my lord," Maura said, wringing her hands. "This is truly awkward. I just wanted to return what belonged to you."

He was swiftly losing his temper. "If I wanted my damn gifts back, why would I go to such effort to have them discreetly returned to your bedchamber?"

"Gifts?" Maura moistened her lips with her tongue. "Did you bother to open the case, Lord Everod?"

He hadn't. All he wanted to do was throw the leather case into the street. It was obvious he had upset her again, but he was getting bloody tired of having his gifts tossed back in his face.

Everod opened the case and paused. His mother's

necklace was coiled within the box. "What is the meaning of this?"

"I thought it was time for me to return the favor and give you a gift. I adore the necklace but I have no right to keep it," she explained, gazing sadly at the box. "I did not even know the necklace belonged to your mother until the earl commented on it."

"Worrington told you." After so many wives, it was amazing that his father even recalled his first countess.

"Once I knew the truth, I could not in good conscience wear it." Maura gestured at the necklace. "You walked away from Worrington Hall with nothing. It isn't much, but I thought you would like to have something of hers."

Everod brushed his thumb over the largest pearl. "Are you attempting to bribe me, Maura?"

Maura huffed in outrage, and leaned back with her arms crossed in front of her. "Me? I would not dare, my lord. I know the only thing that will satisfy you is my blood on your hands. Forgive me, but I am not inclined to accommodate you this morning. If you would step away, I will not bother you again."

Everod hid his grin as he shut the case. Like him, Maura did not care to have her gifts rebuffed. "Come inside. I will thank you properly for your generous gift."

His manservant snorted. Everod would have kicked the man if he had been closer.

"No," she said simply.

Everod had had enough of her haughty demeanor. "Fine. Then I'll join you," he said, climbing into the coach's interior.

"You cannot do this!" she sputtered as he settled in beside her.

"Drive on," Everod ordered the coachman. To her, he asked, "Where are we heading?"

Flabbergasted, Maura gaped at his high-handedness. "The British Museum. I told Abbot I was attending a lecture there."

"Who's Abbot?"

"The family's butler," she replied, probably wondering how she was going to get rid of Everod. "See here, you cannot remain here. We might be seen!"

"How dreadful," he said, feigning dismay. "What will Georgette say?"

"It's what she will *do* to me, if she learns of our meeting!" Maura yelled, unsettled by what she viewed as his unreasonableness.

Curious, Everod cocked his head. "What would dear Aunt Georgette do to you?" He thought of their argument in front of the bookseller's shop. "More importantly, what *did* she do?"

Wordlessly, Maura turned away to gaze out the window. Everod stared hard at her profile. Frowning, he leaned closer, noting that clumsy stroke of powder on her cheekbone. Maura had not worn cosmetics during their previous encounters.

"Christ, she hit you!" Everod cursed Georgette for preying on her niece. The spiteful bitch thought her position as Worrington's countess protected her from all retribution. He was sorely tempted to shatter her arrogant illusion.

Frightened by his demeanor, Maura said, "No. She did not—"

"Still lying for her, I see," Everod said, ruthlessly cutting over her denial. He did not bother to quell his disappointment in her. Maybe he had underestimated her, after all. "Tell me, Maura, did you seek me out for yourself, or are you spying on her behalf?"

"No, you stubborn ingrate!" she shouted, sticking her nose in his face. "I brought you the necklace because *I* wanted you to have something of your mother's. Georgette, had she known the identity of the original owner, would have crushed the pearls with her heel and melted the silver into a thimble!"

Everod placed his finger on her trembling lips to silence her. Surprising both of them, he lowered his head and kissed her. He kept the contact light and undemanding. Maura did not react. Wide-eyed, she stared at him like a startled virgin. The jostling motion of the coach bumped her against him, grinding her lips against his.

"Thank you," he whispered, trailing his lips to kiss the rosy spot where Georgette had slapped Maura for consorting with the man she perceived as the enemy.

Georgette was correct.

He was *her* enemy.

What Maura was to him was—well, that was more complicated.

With a soft sigh, he withdrew and leaned back.

Maura's sea-gray eyes were troubled as she glared at him. "It won't work."

Everod shifted his leg. The subtle swell of his cock contradicted her words. "Do you really want to challenge me, Maura?"

"Gifts . . . a kiss and a little sympathy," she said, becoming angrier as she puzzled out his actions. "I know what you are about, Lord Everod. You think to seduce me?"

"Was that what I was doing?" he drawled lazily. "I must confess *thinking* is rarely involved when I put my hands on a lady." Maura's lower lip pouted so sweetly, Everod was tempted to bite it. When it came to seduction, he rarely played, but was earnest in his intent. "Shall I prove it?"

"Ah, yes. *Les savauges nobles*. You might be surprised to know that your exploits have reached even Worrington Hall," she said, as if she knew everything about him, and condemning him with a few rumors.

Although the stories she had heard were likely true, he did not like being so casually dismissed. "So Georgette was worried that I might return one day," he mused.

"Georgette fears no man," she said smugly. Her loyalty for her aunt made Everod want to throttle Maura until her teeth rattled. "I am not certain, but I think your father hired a man to look into your affairs."

"It must have taken the poor man years to write down all the salacious details." If Everod had been secretly waiting for an olive branch from his father, he had waited in vain. "Did Father read the notes aloud to his countess while they were in bed together?"

Maura chastised him with her eyes. "You hurt him, Lord Everod."

Everod tugged on his cravat, revealing the ugly scar on his neck. "He took his revenge, Maura. Do you really begrudge me mine?"

She offered no rebuttal.

The coach slowed, and finally halted. The coachman opened the door.

"Permit me to pass, my lord."

In spite of his anger and his yearning for revenge, he was reluctant to allow her to escape him so easily. Everod could not deny that his exchanges with Maura stimulated him in several ways, and it left him uncertain on how to proceed. Damn it, he needed more time with her.

Maura stubbornly held his gaze. For several heartbeats, they waged a silent battle of wills, as she patiently waited for him to move aside.

Everod was the first to look away. He nodded at the large building. "I have visited the museum on numerous occasions. It would be an honor to act as your escort."

A shy expression crept into her eyes, and she blushed at his offer. "You? A patron of the museum?" She wrinkled her nose in disbelief. "I doubt you have changed that much in twelve years. It must have involved a wager of some sort."

So maybe he was exaggerating a little. As a boy, he would have rather been playing with wooden swords or riding his horse than sitting indoors with a book. Age had not changed his viewpoint.

"Be daring, Maura," he coaxed, stroking her palm with his finger. "What harm can be done?"

Maura tried not to smile at his attempt at a harmless appeal. "You cannot fool me, Lord Everod. Your reputation precedes you."

"And there was a time when you called me by my name and not my title," he said somberly.

She hesitated. "I—I cannot."

Everod sensed she was wavering, and he took advantage of it. "Share the museum with me, Maura."

CHAPTER 10

Lady Fayre Brawley abhorred gossips. Before she had married her husband, Maccus, Lord Thatcher Standish and his mistress, Lady Hipgrave, had used the *ton*'s insatiable curiosity to publicly attack her. It had been a simply intolerable situation, and if not for her beloved husband, the couple might have succeeded in damaging her reputation beyond repair.

And yet, here she stood just outside Lord and Lady Fancutt's ballroom with Kilby, her dear friend Lady Lyssa, Patience, and one of her closest friends, Callie Mableward, now the happily married Lady Yemant, on the verge of gossiping about one of her brother's friends, Lord Everod.

Nevertheless, the viscount's recent behavior and tragic predicament with his family demanded drastic measures. Lord Everod needed the support of his friends, even if he denied it.

"Which one is she?" Kilby asked, tilting her head as she searched the glittering sea of silk and diamonds.

The five ladies had an excellent view of the ballroom's interior. The overly crowded ballroom had prompted their host, Lord Fancutt, to order the footmen to open all the doors and windows that faced the gardens.

Ramscar's countess, Patience, pointed with her closed fan. "The blonde in the dark green dress is Lady Worrington. I recognize her from the theater."

"Near the column to the right," Patience instructed. "She is chatting with two other ladies. However, I cannot see their faces from this view. Fayre, do you not see Lord Worrington or the young woman?"

Fayre crinkled her nose and shook her head. "No."

Lady Lyssa Nunnick was the eldest daughter of the Duke and Duchess of Wildon. After enduring the humiliation of two failed betrothals in as many years, her parents were desperate for her to marry this season. While Fayre and Kilby had conspired to introduce their friend to many of the eligible bachelors of the *ton,* Lady Lyssa was equally determined to avoid any entanglement.

"Do you think it is wise to meddle in Lord Everod's business?" Lady Lyssa wondered aloud. "As one of *les savauges nobles,* he has never been bothered by gossip or rules. Fayre, you and Kilby know him better than I do. However, I cannot imagine either of your husbands would approve."

"Oh, pish!" Kilby exclaimed, not overly concerned by her husband's disapproval. "Fayne is just as worried about Everod as we are. Unfortunately, men live by some silly code that forbids them to interfere until blood has been drawn or they have been formally asked."

All five ladies sighed in unison. Male reasoning made very little sense to them.

Callie groaned from behind them. Fayre turned and gave her friend a sympathetic pat on her shoulder. She was sitting on one of the stone benches just outside the doors. Rubbing her very swollen belly, her friend would be delivering Lord Yemant's heir within a month.

"Callie, should I summon your husband?" Fayre asked, frowning in concern.

"No," her friend replied, twisting her body to ease the strain on her back. Her warm chocolate-colored eyes reflected the discomfort she was struggling to ignore. "He did not want me to attend Lord and Lady Fancutt's ball this evening because I tire so easily these days. If I ask him to take me home, he will be insufferable to live with."

Fayre moved away from the doorway and sat down next to Callie. "Maccus was the same. He had an apoplectic fit every time I told him I was leaving the house without him. I swear, the man was always telling me to take a nap. Worse, he had my mother agreeing with him!"

"I see her!" Patience said excitedly.

Fayre assisted Callie onto her feet, and all five ladies watched as the mystery lady who was connected to Everod's past joined her aunt. Her brother had told her the lady's name was Maura Keighly.

Miss Keighly was just the sort of lady that would catch the viscount's regard. She was elegantly tall, and moved with an enviable grace. The dress she wore this evening was the height of fashion. Her long dark brown hair was swept up high and a waterfall of curls gleamed as she stood beneath one of the large chandeliers. It was difficult to judge from a distance if she was pretty. However, knowing Everod's taste, Fayre was positive Miss Keighly was stunning.

"She is so slender," Callie sighed, mourning her formerly thin figure.

"And beautiful," Kilby added.

Her brother had been discreetly gathering information about the young lady since Everod was perplexingly sparse on details about her. "Fayne tells me that she is likely brilliant. Her parents are Lord and Lady Courtwill."

Fayre straightened as she noticed her husband and Cadd were sauntering toward Miss Keighly. Lady Fancutt immediately beckoned the gentlemen to come closer while she introduced Lady Worrington and her niece. She ground her teeth as she observed her husband bow gallantly over each lady's extended hand. Did he forget he was married? How dare he flirt with the women!

"Should we despise her on principle?" Patience murmured, sending Fayre a commiserating glance.

"Well, well, what do we have here," Teague Pethum, Viscount Darknell, said, coming up from behind and startling them. "I see five pretty cats who seem to have their claws out this evening. Who is the rat?"

Though Fayre had encountered Lord Darknell at countless functions over the years, the viscount was a close friend of Kilby's. Her brother, on first meeting him, had taken an instant dislike to the gentleman. Fayre had thought the handsome viscount, with his sinfully dark eyes and the hint of silver at his temples, well mannered and rather charming. Fayne, on the other hand, disliked the man because Lord Darknell had once been in love with Kilby. Blood would have likely been spilled, if her sister-in-law had not been wholly in love with Fayne.

"Miss Keighly could hardly be described as a rat," Kilby said, her affection for the gentleman apparent.

"Miss Keighly? Maura Keighly?" Lord Darknell said, peering between Kilby and Lady Lyssa to see the lady.

"Do you know her?" Fayre asked curiously.

The viscount nodded. "In passing. I was introduced to her last evening at the theater."

Lady Lyssa laughed. "Why am I not surprised?"

Kilby made a disappointed sound. "You rogue! You attended last evening, and did not stop by our box?"

Lord Darknell smiled apologetically at the duchess. "I was distracted."

"I am very cross with you!" Kilby said, dismissing him with the haughty tilt of her chin.

"Nunn," he entreated, calling Lady Lyssa the nickname he had given her as a child. "Assist me, if you will."

Lady Lyssa shifted, and aligned herself with her friend. "Honestly, Darknell, do you actually expect me to defend you, when you were likely dallying with your new mistress in some dark corridor?" She sniffed in disdain. "No."

The viscount growled in frustration. The trio had

been friends for many years. The manner in which they provoked each other was reminiscent of how she fought with her older brother. However, when Darknell stared at Lady Lyssa, there was nothing remotely brotherly in his expression. Fayre wondered if the young lady was aware of his interest.

"We are plotting how to save Lord Everod from Miss Keighly," Callie explained to the viscount before he could be further distracted by Kilby and Lady Lyssa.

Lord Darknell raised his eyebrows in surprise. "Really? Good intentions or not, if you ladies want my opinion, I do not think Everod wishes to be rescued."

In unison, six pairs of eyes peered into the ballroom. Everod was standing between Cadd and Miss Keighly. His gaze was fixed keenly on the lady's face. Beside her, Lady Worrington fumed. Unless something was done, the *ton* would be discussing the incident at breakfast.

Oblivious that his friends' wives were avidly observing him, Everod gave Maura a hard look. "You were warned." He was speaking to Cadd, but an appealing blush crept into the young lady's fair complexion.

"I was not aware that certain people were forbidden to me," Maura said, her facial features tight with anger or embarrassment. "Perhaps you could create a list, so these unfortunate mishaps will not occur in the future."

Everod had intended to stay away from Maura

this evening. During the hours they had shared together while they explored each room in the museum, a tentative truce had formed. For a brief time, he had forgotten that he did not trust her, and she had pretended that she did not have a good reason to fear him.

That was, until he saw Cadd hovering at her elbow like a lovesick puppy. Before Solitea and Ramscar could stop him, he had crossed the expanse of the ballroom and separated the chatting couple with his body.

"Everod," Cadd began, recognizing the danger of provoking his friend.

His expression enigmatic, he clasped his hands behind his back. "Very well, Miss Keighly. You may place Lord Byrchmore at the top of the list."

Although Everod had not spared Lady Worrington a single glance, he could feel her sharp beady gaze on him. Neither her husband nor Rowan was nearby to protect them, and she was surely aware that they were being observed by most of the occupants in the ballroom. What was his clever stepmother planning? Would she cry for help? Or had it just occurred to her as she approached him that his influence with the *ton* might be stronger than his father's? For the first time in her selfish life, Georgette was likely bogged down in a mental quandary of indecisiveness.

"Maura, step away from him," Georgette said in a low voice that he was certain dutiful Maura always heeded. "Mr. Brawley . . . Lord Byrchmore . . . Your friend is clearly foxed. It might be prudent to escort Lord Everod back to the card room before he upsets my niece."

He smirked at Lady Worrington's tearful plea. The lady did not give a damn about her niece. She was worried what might happen if Everod turned his attention to her.

Brawley touched him on the arm. "Are you foxed, Everod?"

"No." He had just arrived at the Fancutts' residence, and had gone straight to the card room to greet his friends. If Cadd had not insisted on being introduced to Maura, Everod would have been content to remain there all evening. "Have I upset you, Miss Keighly?" he asked with insincere courtesy.

Maura gave her aunt a side glance. "Alas, no, my lord. This hasn't been one of your better efforts. However, I have complete faith that you will rally with the proper incentive."

Both Brawley and Cadd gawked at her as if she had suddenly sprouted another head. They had expected the lady to cower in his presence; not tweak his nose. Everod's respect for Maura increased as he grinned at her. He liked a lady with mettle.

"Lady Worrington," Maccus Brawley said gently. "It appears your concerns are unfounded. If you do not mind my saying so, your coloring is sallow. If you will permit me, I would be happy to get you something to drink."

The countess blanched at Brawley's insult. "What I want," she said, struggling not to lose her temper in front of so many witnesses. "Is my husband. Maura—"

"Has consented to dance with me," Everod smoothly interjected. "Go find your husband, Lady Worrington.

See if he has the courage you lack to stop me from taking Maura."

Georgette glared at all of them. Afraid of looking
like a fool, she marched off toward the card room in
search of her husband.

As Everod moved toward Maura, Cadd stalled him
by bumping him with his shoulder. "Are you trying to
get Worrington to challenge you?" the marquess demanded, agitated by what he had witnessed. "What
will it take to satisfy you?

"For now," Everod said recklessly. "Just a dance
with Miss Keighly." He bent his head so his breath
teased her ear. "I could be persuaded to do something
utterly wicked if you fancy something more daring."

He presented his arm to Maura.

Begrudgingly, she placed her hand on his forearm.
"Lord Everod?"

"Yes, Miss Keighly."

She exhaled noisily. "You have succeeded in up-
setting me."

Maura avoided meeting anyone's speculative gaze
as she and Lord Everod joined the other
dancers. She had been simply mad to accept his invitation. But what was she to do?

The gentleman she had explored the British Museum with had vanished. Earlier this afternoon, she
had glimpsed the fifteen-year-old young man he had
been as they strolled from room to room. She had enjoyed the museum immensely.

There had been much to admire from artifacts

brought to England by Captain Cook and Captain Byron to several mummies, and Cooper's celebrated portrait of Oliver Cromwell. There were ancient idols from faraway lands, stuffed birds and reptiles, shells, mineral collections, and weapons of the ancient Britons, which Everod had boasted paled when compared to the collection his friend Lord Ramscar had amassed. She had marveled at the banqueting room that displayed a portrait of George II, and a unique table made from different specimens of lava.

Unguarded for once, Everod had offered outrageous opinions on some of the museum's unusual treasures, and to her horror, her laughter echoed at inopportune times. When their stolen hours together had ended, Maura had been melancholy at their parting.

The flirtatious, relaxed manner Everod had exhibited at the museum was gone. In its place was the cynical, mocking Everod she had come to expect. No one had been safe from his grim amusement, not even his friends, Lord Byrchmore and Mr. Brawley. Their offense? They had politely asked their hostess for an introduction. Maura had not immediately recognized the two gentlemen as Everod's friends, until the viscount stepped between her and the men. It had hurt her feelings that she was unworthy of a simple introduction to his friends.

"Smile, Miss Keighly," Everod ordered, bowing to her as the music commenced. "Your admirers are wondering if I have insulted you."

"I have no admirers, my lord," Maura said, rising

from her curtsy. "Or friends here. This is your world. Your friends are concerned for you."

She skipped forward and took his hand.

"Are they?" he murmured, clasping her hand as she circled around him.

When they were face to face, she said, "Mr. Brawley and Lord Byrchmore must be wondering why you are dancing with a lady you have purported to despise. Loyal to you, they worry that you are taunting your father into a public confrontation."

They danced away from each other and came together with another couple. Holding hands, the foursome circled once and separated. Maura changed places with the other lady in her set, and then returned to Lord Everod.

"Your logic has several flaws," he said, as he captured her hand and they moved forward.

She curtsied as he bowed. "How so?"

"I do not despise you, Miss Keighly."

Maura almost stumbled at his declaration. They backed away from each other, and she skipped forward to close the gap between them.

"So you have forgiven me for past offenses?" Maura said, breathless from her exertions. She tried not to be disappointed when he winced at her question. "I thought not."

Everod seized her hand. Maura gasped because it was not part of the dance. "Our situation is more complex than a simple yes or no," he muttered defensively.

From the corner of her eye, Maura saw Lord and Lady Worrington. She did not need to look closely to see that they were furious. Rowan came up to his father and whispered in the earl's ear. The trio watched them as if they expected Lord Everod to toss her over his shoulder and carry her into the dark gardens.

"Hate usually is, Lord Everod."

CHAPTER 11

Hours later, after the Worringtons had departed the ball, the earl stormed into his countess's bedchamber. "You must have ice for blood to sit there so calmly while Everod plots the ruination of our niece!" the earl said from the threshold of his wife's bedchamber.

The cordial he had been imbibing in the library before he had sought her out was slanting dangerously close to the edge of the fine glass. Georgette studied her husband's reflection through the mirror as she calmly brushed her hair. Everod had upset the family again. She viewed his mischief as inconvenient but manageable.

"I will admit, I was initially upset when Everod cornered us in the ballroom," she said, peering sadly at her husband. "However, there is little he can do to us. Once he understands that we will not be intimidated by his presence, he will lose interest in taunting us about the past."

Beneath her serene demeanor, Georgette privately waged a battle with her temper. Everod was determined to spoil her stay in London. Even she had been momentarily stunned by his brazen approach. As he swaggered toward them, there was a possessiveness in her stepson's manner when he stared at Maura that she did not like. By itself, his boorish behavior had not troubled her.

However, Maura was being uncharacteristically difficult these days. And secretive. Georgette had devoted years to building Maura's fear of Everod. As long as she possessed her niece's loyalty, the truth about her liaison with Everod would never be questioned, never be disclosed. Although their discourse with Everod had been brief, Georgette had noted the curiosity in Maura's gaze when she looked at the viscount.

Oh, she could not condemn her niece for being attracted to Everod. Years ago, she herself had been attracted to the then fifteen-year-old young man. Georgette had been ten years older, and a lifetime more cunning. Worrington's heir had effortlessly succumbed to her charms while she indulged her secret fantasies and worshiped his beautiful, perfect body.

The amorous young viscount had been worth the risk she had taken, and with Maura's help, Georgette had been able to banish what she had perceived as a future threat. What she had glimpsed of the man Everod had become only confirmed her fears. Everod was a respectable adversary, one she could not simply discount.

Georgette set her brush on the table and turned to address her husband. "Oh, Worrington, must you pace. I will not have you ill because of this business with Everod."

"By God, the blackguard is arrogant!" the earl

thundered as he sipped his cordial. "Dancing with Maura . . . he was daring me to challenge him!"

It was a situation that Georgette had imagined off and on over the years, but had dismissed because of the unpredictability of the outcome. She stood, and walked over to her husband. The poor man had worked himself into a terrible fit.

"It was one dance. Are you planning to challenge every gentleman who requests a dance from our niece?" she teased, playfully pinching his chin. Earlier, she had also displayed her ire at Maura for that one dance. She had calmed slightly when the young lady had assured her that she had been merely preventing Everod from giving the *ton* a reason to laugh at the Worringtons' narrow-minded prejudice. After all, Everod was not without influential friends.

Georgette embraced the earl. Tilting the glass toward her, she sniffed the dark liquid and wrinkled her nose in distaste. As she had expected, he was sipping cordial. "What you need is one of my tonics, my lord. Your spirits always improve after a glass."

She stepped away and returned to her dressing table. Turning the key, she retrieved the small bottle within the drawer. While her sister had honed her intellect in the sciences, Georgette had focused her keen mind on the subject of plants. Over the years, she had perfected numerous recipes that had benefited her and those that she loved. At the moment, Worrington's health took precedence above all others.

The earl finished his cordial and held out his empty glass. "My spirits are not the only thing your tonics uplift when I imbibe them."

Georgette gave him a sly, intimate smile. "A benefit for me as well."

M aura sat on stone steps that led down into the Worringtons' gardens. The moon was high overhead and there was a chill in the air that made the wool cloak around her shoulders welcome. There was plenty of light blazing within the town house.

Upstairs, she could hear her aunt and uncle arguing. Although their words were unintelligible from where she sat, it was likely her name was being mentioned. After Lord Everod had curtly bowed and walked away from her, Rowan had icily informed her that the family was leaving Lord and Lady Fancutt's ball.

Her ears were still buzzing from her aunt's high-pitched accusations.

"*Did you invite his attentions?*"

"*No, Aunt Georgette.*"

"*This will not do. Everod only seeks to humiliate us.*"

"*Inviting me to dance is neither insulting nor reckless, Aunt. To reject him would only strengthen his resentment toward the family.*"

"*I recall that as a child, you used to chase after young Everod with stars in your eyes, Maura. I pray you have not convinced yourself that Everod's attentions toward you could be honorable.*"

"*No, Aunt.*"

"*Guard your heart, my girl. The viscount thinks only of his pleasures. He would not hesitate to pluck your innocence, and then boast to his friends how eagerly you tumbled!*"

The earl had been satisfied to allow his countess to speak on his behalf. Maura was fortunate that Rowan had arrived at the ball in his own coach. Otherwise, she would have been forced to endure his lectures as well.

The library door quietly opened behind her. Maura twisted her body to address her uninvited companion. Rowan. He had followed them home, after all.

"Good evening, my lord," she said coldly. "If you have come to chastise me over my reckless behavior this evening, then you are too late. I have suffered Aunt Georgette's displeasure for more than an hour, and I am in no mood for another lecture."

"Where is my father?"

"Both Lord and Lady Worrington have retired for the evening," she said, clasping her hands in her lap.

The distant sound of glass being shattered disturbed the tranquility of the night. The earl's gruff voice could be heard, followed by the slam of a door.

"More or less," she said with an indifferent shrug.

A tidy man, Rowan was still dressed in his evening clothes. Removing his handkerchief from his coat, he shook it out and placed it on the hard stone next to her. "Poor, little Maura," Rowan said sympathetically as he stiffly settled in beside her. He exhaled noisily. "Georgette can be quite ruthless when crossed."

Maura scowled at the shadowed gardens. "It was one dance in a crowded ballroom. Your father and my aunt are behaving as if I had been discovered disheveled in one of Lord Fancutt's bedchambers with your brother."

"It would not be a first for my brother," Rowan muttered under his breath.

"Oh, what do you know of your brother's life?" she demanded, unwilling to hear another slur against Everod. "You were thirteen when he left Worrington Hall. I highly doubt you have disobeyed your father's dictates by visiting your elder brother, and getting to know the man he has become."

Maura could not prevent the disdain from creeping into her inflection. Rowan was a decent, honorable man. He had always treated her kindly. Nevertheless, Worrington's second son believed he was born to rule over his inferiors, and there were occasions when his condescension made her teeth ache.

"Is that what you are trying to do, Maura? *Know* my brother?"

She jumped to her feet, and whirled around to face him. "Your remark was unbelievably rude, even for you, *Mr.* Lidsaw!" She never addressed him formally unless she was extremely vexed with him. Unfortunately, since her arrival in London, it took little effort on Rowan's part to annoy her.

Rowan hastily rose up, determined to calm her. "Maura, your aunt and my father are concerned. Georgette fears any old affection you may be harboring for my brother has blinded you to his faults."

She flinched as if Rowan had struck her. Were her tender feelings for Worrington's heir twelve years earlier so obvious to everyone, including Everod? Oh, how they all must have laughed at her!

"I think hate has blinded all of you," she replied angrily. "Your brother has done nothing untoward except remind you all that he has survived without the benevolence of his family."

"I notice that you are careful to distance yourself from the family when you hurl accusations at us." He grabbed her by the elbows when she did not respond. "Lest you forget, my lady, you took part in what transpired twelve years ago. It was *your* tearful accusations that sent my father out of the house in search of his traitorous son. It was *you* who clutched your aunt's hand while you confirmed Georgette's tale that she had been attacked by my brother in the garden. Is that really what happened, Maura? Did your young innocent eyes witness the painful violation of a man's lust and domination over your beloved aunt?"

No.

Even now, she could not vocalize the depth of her betrayal to Lord Everod. How could she explain to anyone how she felt that day when she followed Everod into the gardens with her aunt? Crouched behind a flowering bush, she had watched with hurt and surprise as her aunt had exposed her breast, and then invited the fifteen-year-old Everod to taste. The young viscount had touched Georgette, and her aunt had not protested.

Until later.

Later, when Everod thrashed in his bed with a festering cut on his throat, and senseless with fever. In those dark hours, Georgette had summoned Maura to her bedchamber and begged her for her help.

"Oh, my treasure, I do not know what to do. I have lost Worrington after this treachery," Georgette sobbed.

"Uncle will forgive you."

"No, Maura, he will not," the older woman said,

her tears seeping silently from the corners of her eyes. Georgette struggled for composure. "I realize now that you followed us into the gardens, Maura. I understand how it must have looked—"

"You tugged on your bodice, and bared your breast," Maura said accusingly, her own heart aching because Everod preferred her aunt. "You begged him to kiss you!"

"Wrong! He threatened me," Georgette yelled, so genuinely appalled that Maura wondered if she had misunderstood the situation. "Everod accused me of seducing one of the grooms. He promised not to tell Worrington, but I had to . . . oh, my dearest Maura, you have no notion of the evil a man can do to a lady. What you thought you saw, what I did, was not by choice. Everod had bribed the servant to testify against me. I only acted to protect my husband. My marriage."

Had she been wrong? Her aunt had cried out Everod's name several times. Had Georgette been begging him to stop? Maura had been horrified by the violence committed to Everod. She had blamed herself and her aunt. Perhaps Everod had brought this tragedy upon himself. Unsure, Maura sat on the edge of her aunt's bed.

Georgette took her hand, and placed it on her stomach. "I have a secret. I can tell no one but you, my treasure. I fear Everod's lust has taken root, Maura. A child may result from his violence." Her aunt buried her face in Maura's shoulder and sobbed. "I will lose my husband."

Maura hugged her aunt. Georgette's entire body

was quaking as her worst fears took hold. "Lord Wor-
rington loves you. He would not blame you when the
sin belongs to his son."

Her aunt froze in her embrace. "As long as the sin
points to Everod, and not me," Georgette whispered in
Maura's ear. She wet her dry lips. "You could help
me, Maura. You were there with us. You could tell your
uncle the truth."

"The truth?" she echoed faintly.

Growing in confidence, Georgette pulled away
and nodded eagerly. "You could protect me. Us. Pro-
tect my unborn child from Worrington's wrath. You
could tell everyone that you saw Everod attack me.
The earl would believe you. You could convince him
that there was nothing I could do to stop his son from
hurting me."

Maura started, realizing Rowan still cradled her in
his embrace. "Release me," she said, not waiting for
him to comply. She tugged away, and hugged herself.

"Maura, come back here!" Rowan said, as he followed her down the steps.

Blood protects blood.

Georgette had said the phrase to her the day Everod
was banished from his own house and family. Maura
had tried to protect her aunt from Worrington's anger.
She had even believed her lies for a time. It was painless when no one mentioned Everod's name. He had
ceased to exist for the family.

Five years later, the extent of Georgette's deception surfaced during an unrelated conversation Maura
had with her mother. With the incident involving
Everod and her aunt forgotten, Maura had casually

mentioned that it was a pity that Georgette and Lord Worrington were childless. Her aunt had always been generously attentive her. Maura had told her mother that she believed Georgette would be a doting mother.

Her mother paused in her stitching, and looked questioningly at her daughter. "I am pleased to hear that your aunt treats you well during our absence. However, my sister will never hold her own child in her arms."

Lady Courtwill had spoken so matter-of-factly that Maura had gaped at her. "How can you be so certain, Mama? You and Papa were married for many years before I was born."

Maura could see that her mother was uncomfortable with the subject. She quietly stitched for several minutes before her mother spoke again. "My sister is barren, Maura."

"No," she said, her heart welling with pity for Georgette. *Perhaps that was the reason her aunt insisted that Maura visit her each summer. For a few months, she could pretend that she had a child to love. "How could fate be so cruel?"*

Lady Courtwell stabbed her needle into her thumb. Setting aside her embroidery, she brought the tiny wound to her lips. "Fate did not make my sister barren, Maura," she said, her voice laced with irritability. "Georgette was responsible. While married to Lord Perton, she learned that she was carrying another man's child, and promptly took steps to rid herself of the babe." The countess noted her daughter's face and frowned. "Dear child, this was not the first time my sister denied herself the joy of being a mother. It was,

however, her last. An infection set in, and when Geor-
gette recovered, she understood that she would never
carry another child in her womb again."

It was then her aunt's tearful words whispered in
her mind.

"I have a secret. I can tell no one but you, my trea-
sure. I fear Everod's lust has taken root, Maura. A
child may result from his violence."

If what her mother had revealed was true, then
Georgette had lied to Maura. Her aunt had known there
was no chance Everod or any man could have gotten
her with child. She had used the possibility of a child
to sway Maura, to coax her into believing that Georgette was protecting more than just herself with her
lies. From that day onward, Maura had viewed what
occurred between Everod and her aunt differently.

Even so, nothing changed.

There was no point in confronting her aunt. Everod
was gone, his face and voice had faded in her memories. The damage wrought to the family could not be
undone. Untangling one lie would create new problems for her aunt and uncle. Maura did not want to
bear the responsibility of ruining their marriage because of what her mother had told her.

"Did you hear what I said, Maura?" Rowan demanded, bringing her back to the present, back to him.

"What do you want from me, Rowan?" She backed
away when he took a step forward. "I am not pretending that I am any less responsible for what happened
to your brother the day I found him with Aunt Georgette. I just feel Lord Everod has paid a high price for
something that is best forgotten. I refuse to punish

him further." Her guilt felt like ballast, a persistent companion, but Rowan was not the one who could absolve her from the lies she had told.

Only Everod.

However, he was a hardened man who had no forgiveness in his heart. Not for her, not for anyone.

Maura saw a glint as Rowan's teeth flashed as he smiled in relief. "Good." At her bewildered expression, he continued, "What I meant to say is, I hope my brother's notorious exploits have not soured you toward all the gentlemen in my family."

She suddenly was aware Rowan was less interested in discussing the past than she was. The gentleman wanted to discuss their future. Until this moment, she had carefully avoided being alone with him. The darkness could not conceal Rowan's earnest determination to press his intentions.

"It is late," she said, praying his courage would wane and he would just leave.

Understanding lit his shadowed gaze. "Of course. It has been a difficult evening."

"Thank you for understanding," she said, strolling toward the stairs.

Rowan politely grabbed her elbow and guided her up the steps. "And, Maura?"

"Yes—mmm-umph!"

Rowan crushed his mouth over hers. His kiss was so unexpected, all Maura could do was stand there. His mouth pushed at her lips, demanding a response. Regrettably, Maura's experience with kisses was limited. She did not know how to properly respond.

Rowan pulled away, and looked rather pleased

with his efforts. "Pleasant dreams," he said, his sly expression revealing that he hoped that she would be thinking of him.

Flummoxed, Maura did not walk with him to the door. She raised her hand in a tentative wave of farewell, as Rowan entered the house. He would not bother Lord Worrington at this late hour. Maura expected he would go home.

"Well, well . . . it appears Little Brother has declared himself," Everod said, causing her to shriek a musical note so high it was practically inaudible. "Rather sloppily, I might add. You have drool on your chin."

CHAPTER 12

"What are you doing here?"

Unrushed, Everod retrieved a handkerchief from his pocket and offered it to Maura. She would have to be very brave and come to him if she wanted the neatly pressed linen.

He grinned when she marched down the steps and snatched the handkerchief from his outstretched hand.

She dabbed at her mouth and chin. Crushing the linen in her hand, she shook her finger at him. "How long have you—? Ooooph . . . How dare you eavesdrop on a private conversation!" she said, indignant that he might have witnessed more than his brother kissing her.

Maura had no clue how lovely she was with her eyes flashing like lightning warning of an approaching storm, her cheeks rosy, and the saucy bobble of her corkscrew curls as she cocked her head challengingly at him. He wanted to push back the heavy cloak that was concealing her neck and nibble.

"Should I have revealed myself to Rowan?"

At her horrified expression, he nodded. "I thought not. Besides, I was intrigued how Rowan planned to discourage you from seeing me when he plans to lure you into his bed."

"Your brother hopes to marry me!" she said, before she could ponder the wisdom of revealing Rowan's aspirations to Everod.

His gut lurched at her revelation. She had only confirmed what he had already suspected. "Marriage, you say. Someone has high ambitions. Is it you, Rowan, or your aunt?"

Maura bit her lip, belatedly realizing she had confessed too much. So Georgette was determined to marry her niece to Rowan, was she? The greedy wench was single-minded when it came to getting her claws into all the Lidsaw men.

"When will the banns be posted?" Everod purred with soft menace. He was angry at Georgette. His hatred of the countess would never burn itself out. However, he was also furious at Maura. Was she as ambitious as her aunt or simply blinded by her loyalty?

He had overheard her words to Rowan. She had claimed that unlike the rest of his family, she no longer intended to punish Everod for his past sins. Everod hungered to test the young lady's resolve.

"N-nothing has been decided," Maura stuttered as he closed in, forcing her to circle around and back into the shadows in order to keep a respectable distance.

What Maura did not comprehend was that she was being cleverly maneuvered, and Everod was already anticipating the moment when he sprung the trap.

Maura glanced upward at the darkened windows on the upper stories. It appeared both her aunt and uncle had retired to their separate bedchambers. She was utterly alone with Everod.

"Really?" the viscount taunted, edging closer as he circled around her. "Georgette covets the union between you and my brother, so it is highly probably that my father supports the marriage as well. Rowan also agrees, which explains his clumsy attempt at seduction. The only one who seems indecisive is you."

"What of you?" she asked in a hushed whisper. Her cloak concealed most of her body, but her delicate features glowed like warm cream in the moonlight. "Would you approve of the match?"

"Are you asking for my blessing, Maura?" He wrapped one of her curls around his finger, and gently tugged her head back so the back of her head rested on his upper chest.

"No."

"Good. You won't be getting it," he said, his fingers spearing through her hair. "Rowan is the wrong gent for you."

With his fingers entangled in her hair, Maura could not move out of reach without hurting herself. She closed her eyes, and viewed his closeness, his caresses as a test. He was gloveless, and she felt his nails scrape her scalp. Maura shivered. "A bold statement, Lord Everod."

"Do you think so?" He buried his nose into her hair, and inhaled deeply.

She had never felt a man's body aligned so intimately against hers, as if they were two pieces of one whole being. One of his hands glided down from her hair, and moved slowly until it rested on her left hip. Everod made no attempt to slip his hand between the folds of her cloak. Still, it burned like a brand through the layers of her clothing.

What had they been discussing? Maura frantically searched for the fraying threads of their earlier conversation, one neither of them seemed interested in finishing. All she could think about was his hand on her hip, and what he planned to do next.

"Strangers," Maura blurted out, when she felt the tip of his tongue trace her ear. The stars beneath her eyelids were brighter than the ones she glimpsed in the night's sky. "You c-cannot reject the likelihood of marriage involving two people that you scarcely know."

His fingers flexed on her hip as he coaxed her face upward with his other hand until her lips hovered inches from his. "I do not have to befriend my brother to understand that you do not want him."

Maura opened her eyes. Her throat felt parched, and her tongue sluggish as she stared longingly into Everod's amber-green gaze. "I—"

"Hush," he said, nipping her lower lip to chastise her. "No more lies. Better still, I dare you to prove me wrong."

Prove him wrong? How was she supposed to convince him when her feelings for Rowan were so conflicted? Of course she loved Everod's younger brother. Theirs was an affection born of familiarity, family, and years of friendship. What secretly worried Maura was the lack of passion between her and Rowan. The man had treated her like a brother for years, and now the family was urging them to marry. Her aunt believed all Maura desired was a proper courtship from Rowan, when what she really needed was time to muddle her way to her own conclusion.

"Why are you here? What do you want from me?" she asked, a part of her fearful of his answer.

His smile did little to reassure her. It reminded her of a large ravenous beast, who was preparing to devour her. *"This."*

E verod slanted his mouth over Maura's lips, effectively silencing her protest. If he had told Maura what he wanted in crude unseemly terms, she would have shoved him away and run into the sanctuary she thought Worrington's town house provided. What the lady had not guessed was that there was no haven he could not breach if he desired.

And desire burned within him now.

He had only tarried in the gardens with the hope of glimpsing her from the window. Maura had made it ridiculously easy for him when she strolled into the gardens to avoid listening to Lord and Lady Worrington's argument. Rowan's appearance and parting kiss had sealed the lady's fate. Everod would not be satisfied with a single kiss as his younger brother had been.

Releasing her lips, he stared broodingly down at her. Maura's lips were parted as she panted quietly. Her sensitive skin was unused to a man's impatience. Already, her lips were slightly fuller and gleamed as if dipped in nectar. Everod had barely sampled the sweetness of her luscious mouth, and he hungered for more.

He spun her around. Instinctively, Maura placed

her hands on his chest to prevent him from pressing intimately against her. Unbeknownst to her, his cock filled his breeches like an iron bar. He longed to rub the rigid length down the cleft of her bare buttocks, and watch her tremble in anticipation. When he had her begging and wild with need, he wanted to part her sweet thighs and plunge his cock into her drenched sheath as he took her from behind.

"You cannot be frightened of my kisses," he said, shackling her wrist and dragging her to his chest.

She struggled to free her wrists, but soon understood that he was not finished with her. "I never said I was," was her haughty reply.

Everod pulled her deeper into the gardens. He had played there as a boy, and did not need much more than the moon to light his way. "Of course you are," he teased, spinning her around until she was light-headed. "Of course you are." He caught her by the waist. "I know your secret, Maura Keighly." He bent his head to her ear. "Shall I tell you what you have not told a living soul?"

Maura shook her head in mute denial.

He had slipped his hands under her cloak, enjoying the warmth and female curves the garment concealed. "You fear my kisses because you desire them above all others."

She made a scoffing noise at his smug declaration.

Keeping her tightly pressed against him with one hand, he cupped her cheek with the other. He sensed she was biding time in hopes that he would grow careless, thus giving her a chance to escape.

Everod might on occasion be impulsive, but he was not neglectful with what he considered his. "You wanted me to kiss you this afternoon," he said, brushing his mouth teasingly over hers.

"I had no such wish. You, Lord Everod, are delusional!" she said, straining against him to avoid his questing lips.

"You used to call me by name. As if we were—"

"Brother and sister!" she hissed, unaware that her squirming was inflaming him more than her earlier submissiveness.

"Lovers." Everod ended her defiance by overwhelming her with another bruising kiss. "Say my name. Just once. Your tongue will not blacken and rot if you grant me this indulgence."

He had not given anyone leave to use his Christian name in twelve years. "Townsend" was a family name on his mother's side. The surname dated back to the fifteenth century. Like his dear mother, the descendants from the noble lineage had perished long ago. Maura had been one of the few individuals who had not called him by his title. After he had been cast aside by his family, he had become Everod. Any lover foolish enough to risk calling him by his first name would have sorely regretted her boldness.

Until now.

Everod wanted to hear Maura whisper his name. "Have you forgotten it?"

Maura hesitated. "If I say your name, will you permit me to return to the house?"

He nuzzled her cheek to prevent her from glimpsing

the triumph in his gaze. She thought to bargain with him, when she had already lost the battle. Everod could only marvel at her naivety. "You have my word," he promised solemnly as he released her.

Confident that she had won, she took a step backward to place some distance between them. "Very well." It was then that she noticed he had lured her farther from the house than she had assumed. "Townsend," she said pleasantly, nodding her head as if she expected him to behave like a trained dog performing at Astley's.

Maura had much to learn about him.

Everod did not step aside. "Forgive me, but after twelve years, I expected something more," he said apologetically.

"More?" she asked warily.

He gestured vaguely. "More intimacy. More passion."

"More's the pity, I lack both." Maura tried to dismiss him by walking around him. He lazily caught her wrist and tugged her to his side. She was not leaving until he was finished with her.

"Lying scoundrel!" She seethed at what she perceived as deception on his part. "You swore that I could return to the house once I uttered your name."

"And I will keep my promise," he said soothingly. "Eventually."

Maura wanted to kick something for being tricked. Everod was having too much fun to allow her to escape so easily. Worse still, it was pride that was spurring her anger and stubbornness. She did not want to leave him. Duty and responsibility awaited her in the Worrington household. Everod had always represented freedom and adventure. Maura had not realized until she had seen him again, how much she missed him.

Alone in the gardens with Everod, she found it effortless to believe there was something magical about the night. *What harm comes from a few stolen kisses?* her mind whispered enticingly. When the sun rose, the fragile truce she and Everod shared would evaporate with the morning dew and the cold stranger would return. The man who considered her the enemy, though her heart fiercely rejected the notion.

"Come now, Maura. It is unlike you to give up without a fight," he said, stalking her until she bumped up against one of the stone walls segmenting the garden. "Perhaps if you say my name and kiss me sweetly on the lips, I may be content to let you run off to your warm bed."

"*More* games, my lord?" she asked tartly.

Everod laughed, appreciating her wit. "Yes, love. Most scoundrels love to play wicked games. Are you brave enough to risk losing your virtue to me?"

Something dark and foreign pooled in her loins. Maura shivered. "Touch me, and I will scream," she threatened.

"Without a doubt," he said, his swift agreement sounding suspiciously like a promise. "So are you going to kiss me, lovely Maura, or do you want me to make you?"

She gasped at his impropriety. "Are you completely without scruples?"

"Undeniably." He braced his arms against the stone, caging her with his embrace. "And you are delaying the inevitable, Maura Keighly."

The kiss.

"Oh, very well," she said ungraciously, huffing as if it would be a great hardship to suffer the caress of his mouth. "Bend down. My neck cracks every time I—"

Everod picked her up and plopped her bottom on the top portion of the waist-high wall. "I may lack scruples, but I loathe inconveniencing a lady willing to kiss me."

He was laughing at her again. His amber-green eyes gleamed, daring her to be reckless.

Kiss him.

Later, she would not be able to comfort herself with the knowledge that he had forced her. Maura straightened her shoulders as she prepared to show him that she was not afraid of him or his bone-melting kisses.

Using her hands to balance herself on the stone wall, Maura leaned forward, her lips slightly parted. Everod was poised directly in front of her, his arms crossed. His condescending smirk told her that he believed that she lacked the courage. Well, she would show him!

Maura toppled off her precarious perch. She would have fallen headlong onto the ground, if Everod had not caught her to him. He grunted as her outstretched hands hit him in the chest. Maura seized his cravat and pulled his head down until his mouth covered hers.

The sounds of the night seemed to fade away as she favored his lips with soft, moist pecks. Everod moaned against her mouth. Encouraged, Maura's fingers released his cravat and moved higher, finding purchase around the viscount's neck. He tightened his hold and her lips parted in surprise at his strength. Everod took advantage of the breach. A conqueror at heart, Everod speared his tongue into the moist recesses of her mouth, claiming and teasing her to respond.

Her body instinctively understood. Heat spread over her breasts as she felt her nipples harden into painful points against her corset. Maura lightly brushed her tongue against his, and the intimate caress made her dizzy with excitement. A longing was building within her, threatening to burst if she did not seek relief. The sensation bordered on pain, making her restless as she strained her body against him. Maura wanted something more from him. Whatever it was, it was more dangerous than a simple kiss.

She slowly, reluctantly, pulled away. "Townsend," she murmured, her husky voice filled with wonderment. Maura smiled up into his face, shaken by the desire of wanting to kiss him again.

"Ah, lady, you tempt me," he sighed.

Instead of accepting her unspoken invitation, Everod lowered her until her feet were firmly on the ground again. With the impersonal touch of a handmaid, he briskly brushed her skirts back into place.

He was letting her go.

After the fiery passion of their shared kiss, Everod's rejection stung. "Did I do something wrong?"

"Your dedication to the task was admirable. Consider our bargain fulfilled. You may return to the house as I had promised," he said. His limbs seemed rigid as he coaxed her away with a not-so-subtle shove in the proper direction.

She should be grateful. Everod had clearly grown weary of teasing her, and now was content to send her away. Maura tried not to pout, but she was hurt the kiss meant little to him. While the night concealed her private mortification caused by his dismissal, she was equally frustrated that his expression was shrouded by the shadows.

Maura walked away from him and then halted. "Were you not pleasured by our kiss?" She winced, furious that the slight wobble in her inflection revealed more than she desired. "No, do not answer. It was a foolish question. Good evening, Lord Everod."

She had heard ladies whispering about him. He had kissed a legion of women, had bedded a score or more. Why would one awkward kiss at midnight mean anything to a scoundrel like him?

He grabbed her by the arm, and pulled her back into his embrace before she reached the steps to the terrace. His hand cupped the back of her head as he forced Maura to look up at him. "You seem so innocent," he mused, his amber-green eyes glowing with an inner fire as he studied her face. "It seems impossible, knowing your deceitful aunt had a hand in raising you. Georgette abhors anything she can never hope to attain. She corrupts out of spite."

"My lord, although I love my aunt, I am not *her*," Maura said evenly.

"Innocent or deceitful temptress . . . I am not certain the truth will alter our fate," he said, sliding his hand down her left arm until he captured her hand. Everod brought her hand, not to his heart as she had expected, but to the apex of his breeches. Maura would have recoiled if he had not held her hand, making her caress the unyielding bulge of his arousal.

"A woman's pleasure is a powerful aphrodisiac," he murmured, nuzzling the top of her head with his chin. "If a mere kiss arouses me, I look forward to stretching you out on my bed and fucking you until there is no doubt in your curious brain that I was well pleasured."

Maura snatched her hand away from his breeches, away from the rigid, scorching length he intended to plunder her body with if she lingered in his company. "I am not one of your mistresses," she said, edging away from him. "A lady you can dally with for a time and discard on a whim. I am a nobleman's daughter. An innocent."

He shrugged nonchalantly. "Innocent or not, our differences will not matter. Verily, you will squirm like any other greedy wench who has a passionate gent betwixt her thighs. You will claw and beg, shouting my name as I bury myself over and over into your clinging, tight wetness until we burn out the ravenous need that simmers just beneath the surface."

Maura trembled as the unbidden image of them coupling shimmered in her mind. It was her misfortunate that she understood the ravenous need that Everod spoke of. Like the man before her, its mysterious nature and tantalizing promises of rapturous delight and adventure beckoned her to be daring. She had felt nothing more than annoyance when Rowan kissed her. Why did his elder brother effortlessly fascinate her? Whether he sought revenge or simply his own pleasure, Lord Everod was not the sort of gentleman a decent lady married. To love him would only lead to a broken heart.

Love.

Oh, God! Had she already fallen in love with the scoundrel? Without a word, Maura dashed up the steps as fast as she could manage in her long skirts, and slipped into the house. She could hear Everod softly chuckle at her hasty retreat.

"Dream of me, sweet lady."

His last words taunted her until exhaustion finally claimed her.

CHAPTER 13

I had hoped that you would find your way here," Fayne Carlisle, Duke of Solitea, said, opening his door to Everod. "Cadd and Ram had planned to visit Moirai's Lust and a few of your favorite haunts to see if they could catch up with you."

Everod removed his hat, and combed his hair back with his hand. "Some of my favorite places are not fit for a married gent like Ram. His countess will likely try to castrate me if her man runs into trouble."

Or one of my former mistresses.

The two men headed for the library. It was two o'clock in the morning. In a matter of hours, the servants would be stirring from their beds. For as long as Everod could recall, there wasn't an hour in which his friend had not opened the door for him. He valued Solitea's friendship, and the sense of family the Carlisles had tried to bring to his life.

"Where is your duchess?" He kept his voice low until they entered the library. He did not want to awaken the household.

"Asleep." Solitea gestured to the decanter of brandy, but Everod shook his head. He did not need his thoughts muddled any more than they were.

"The babe makes her tire easily, and the stomach sickness has been striking her at odd moments," Solitea explained, his green eyes reflecting his private worries about the lady who was his entire world. "She despises what she perceives as weakness in herself. Gypsy tries to be helpful, but that girl has a talent for turning the simplest task into utter chaos."

Clearly recalling some of Gypsy's most recent mischief, the duke laughed as he collapsed on the sofa. He placed his hand on his chest as if he could prevent his lungs from bursting. If the man grieved for his old bachelor ways, he hid it well. Everod had not seen his friend so content.

"What about you?" Solitea asked, his merriment dimming as he reached from behind to tuck a pillow under his head. "Brawley arrogantly lectured me about my negligence for allowing you to leave the card room."

Everod sneered. "Brawley can be an arse!"

"That's true," his friend concurred, unperturbed that his brother-in-law had been insulted. "What galls me is the fact that he was correct. You gave me the impression after that small incident at the theater that you planned to stay away from the Worringtons, and that young lady—Oh, what was her name? Mary?" He made a vague gesture with his hand.

"Maura . . . Maura Keighly," Everod said, not believing his friend had forgotten Maura's name or her connection to the family. The man was quicker than all *les sauvages nobles* combined. "Worrington's niece by marriage."

Solitea pinned him with a direct stare. "And what

is she to you? Cadd remarked that there was nothing cousinly about your posturing around Miss Keighly. He also—"

The reminder of Cadd's interest in Maura rekindled Everod's anger toward his friend. "I have heard enough of Cadd's bloody observations. If he has any sense, he will stay out of my way for several days. I warned the man off, and he thought nothing of wheedling an introduction from Lady Fancutt."

"There is something going on with the niece," Solitea said, closing his eyes. "You caused quite a stir with the Worringtons when you danced with her."

He could not decide which gave him the greatest pleasure, Maura's defiance of the family by consenting to dance with him or watching his father, Rowan, and Georgette seethe in fury at his boldness. "My little brother seemed ready to challenge me for daring to touch Maura's hand. The puppy fancies himself in love. You should have seen how he slobbered all over her, when he—"

Solitea opened one eye. "No."

"No? No, what?" Everod leaned forward to drag a second chair closer so he could prop his long legs on it.

Solitea opened both eyes and scowled at him. "Tell me you did not follow the Worringtons back to their town house. Or trespass onto the grounds."

"The town house is mine," Everod said, settling back in his chair. "Or will be once Worrington grants me my fondest wish by dying soon."

Everod belatedly recalled only two years had passed since Solitea had inherited the dukedom from his father. The old duke had died suddenly, and his friend still grieved over the family's loss.

"Don't jest about such things," Solitea said, his eyes narrowing with anger. "You may never be able to forgive Worrington for his callous treatment, but he's still your father. Besides, I know you, Everod. You don't want the man's blood on your hands."

"You credit me with benevolence I lack inside of me," he replied carelessly. "No, cease the lecture. I have no ambition to face either my father or brother over pistols at dawn. Why should I inconvenience myself when the Worringtons have provided me an amusing and pretty distraction?"

"Miss Keighly."

Everod slouched and braced his head up with his fist against his cheek. "You sound like you disapprove."

"Seducing virgins for amusement is a blood sport I have never fancied," Solitea growled, reminding Everod that he never wanted to make the young duke his enemy. "I would have happily bathed in Lord Thatcher Standish's blood for seducing my sister, but Fayre was so humiliated, so hurt by the bastard's betrayal, that she begged Father and me not to retaliate."

Everod grew quiet.

He had forgotten about Lady Fayre's ill-fated love affair with Standish. Solitea rarely mentioned the incident. The Carlisle family had managed to quell most of the rumors, and dismissed Standish's cruel boasts as lies. In a matter of weeks, another scandal had replaced the *ton*'s interest in Solitea's sister.

His friend broke the awkward silence between them. "Seducing Miss Keighly will not satisfy you."

Everod thought about Maura's innocent lips rubbing and nibbling his. She was completely inept at her task, but his body did not seem to care. He had been so aroused all he wanted to do was shove her against the wall and lose himself in all her feminine softness. He grinned mockingly at his loss of control.

"I disagree," he said, covering his yawn with the back of his hand. "A willing Maura Keighly in my bed could make me very tolerant to the Worringtons. She's very devoted to my father. I wonder, would she sacrifice her virginity for him?"

Or guilt.

Would she surrender her body to appease him for the lies she told to protect her aunt?

"It is a distasteful notion," his friend spat, sitting up from his reclining position. "Stick to your usual fare of widows and courtesans, Everod. This vengeful course is beneath you. Miss Keighly does not deserve to be the sacrificial lamb for the Worringtons' treachery."

Pride kept him silent, though a part of him agreed with Solitea. If he had been completely void of the scruples Maura had accused him of lacking, Everod would have taken Maura's innocence this evening. He sensed her awareness of him, her curiosity. When he had sent her away after she had kissed him, Maura had been hurt by his dismissal. If he had lingered in the gardens with her, he was confident that the lady would have granted him further liberties.

"If I bed Miss Keighly, I promise the lady will be willing," he said, attempting to assure his friend that he was not an utter scoundrel.

"You forget I have seen you charm a reluctant

lady," Solitea said, unimpressed. "I have no doubt Miss Keighly will think she had a choice."

Unbeknownst to both men, Kilby Carlisle, Duchess of Solitea, crept away and sagged against the table just beyond the open door that led to the library. She was distressed by what she had overheard. She initially had planned to reveal herself to her husband and Everod and join them in the library. That was, until she heard Miss Keighly's name. She adored Lord Everod as much as her husband, but this business with Maura Keighly was wrong. Fayne loved Everod. He would not interfere, unless blood was spilled, and even then, he would support his friend. Who would protect Miss Keighly from Everod? It appeared the poor young lady needed a few friends. For the first time, Kilby refused to align herself with her husband.

It wasn't until morning that Maura discovered why Everod had paid a visit to the town house. The leather case in her hands was proof that he had been in the house. Maura had discovered it hidden behind the folding support of the small reading table in her chamber. If she had not decided to read several pages from Mrs. Radcliffe's book this morning, it might have been days before she had noticed the case.

When she opened the case, the mystery as to why Everod had not simply left the case on her dressing table was solved. Maura plopped down on the chair. Within the padded interior rested not only his mother's silver and pearl necklace, but matching earrings, two bracelets, and a narrow silver ring. It was the complete suite. He had possessed the other pieces all along. No wonder he had been annoyed when he saw the missing necklace around her neck that evening at the theater.

Why had he given his mother's jewelry to her?

Maura had harbored no ill will in surrendering the necklace to him. It was a keepsake of his mother's, after all. She picked up the delicate silver band, and admired the three medium-sized pearls embedded in the scrolling design. Everod's generosity confused her. Placing the open case on the reading table, she slid the ring down the third finger of her right hand.

It fit her perfectly.

She started at the sudden knock at her door. Fearing her aunt might be on the other side of the door, Maura hastily closed the lid on the jewelry case and returned it to its hiding place behind her book. She flinched at the next series of firm knocks. Belatedly, she recalled the silver ring on her hand, but if someone questioned her about it, she could always tell them that it had been a gift from her mother.

Maura opened the door and was surprised to see the family butler, Abbot, on the other side. "I beg your pardon, Abbot, I was, uh, distracted," she finished lamely.

"Forgive me for disturbing you, Miss Keighly," the butler said politely. "Three ladies have come calling, and request an audience with you. Her Grace said that it was imperative that she meet with you this afternoon."

"Me?" she squeaked, wishing she had chosen a prettier gown for the afternoon. "Are you certain? There must be a mistake."

"Her Grace, the Duchess of Solitea, and her companions referred to you by name, Miss Keighly." He glanced questioningly at her when she began to back away. His normally formal demeanor softened with sympathy. "Under their fancy titles and dresses, those ladies are simple kindhearted lasses like you, I expect. I will have Cook send up some refreshments to the drawing room while you tidy yourself."

Abbot bowed and pulled the door closed.

Oh, my, Maura thought as she picked up her comb and peered into the small looking glass on her dressing table. A duchess was waiting for her in the Worringtons' drawing room! Aunt Georgette would be thrilled when she learned that her niece was not spending all her time with her nose in a book.

By the time Maura had reached the stairs, her anticipation of meeting the three ladies had dimmed somewhat. She could not recall being introduced to the Duchess of Solitea, though the title seemed familiar. Perhaps Aunt Georgette had begged a favor from an acquaintance, and the young ladies had been asked to befriend Maura.

The prospect that the Duchess of Solitea had called on her out of pity doused the remaining embers of her excitement. With her shoulders set, and her head held high, Maura entered the drawing room.

E verod, I am honored that you have an hour or so to spare for your old friends these days," Velouette said, extending her hand in greeting as she reclined on a brilliant gold chaise longue near the window.

"I was under orders to see you. Our mutual friend Lady Silver tells me that you have rejected all of her invitations to join her, Vel," Everod said, making a soft tsking noise. "It is unlike you to barricade yourself in your house at the height of the social season."

Lady Silver and Lady Spryng had both formed intimate albeit brief connections with several of *les sauvages nobles*. The merry widows were outrageous and flirtatious, and oftentimes more daring than most gents. One night, the pair had offered to share him, when Solitea, the pompous arse, had cried off. The ladies had sated his every whim, leaving him smugly content and exhausted. They had been the ones to dub him "Everhard," much to his amusement. To this day, the fond memory of that night could make his cock twitch if he dwelled on it.

"Everod, I am hardly fit to walk through a door," Velouette said, her eyes filling with self-pitying tears. She was prepared this time, and retrieved her lace handkerchief from her sleeve. "Look at me! I am as round as a gooseberry in this dress! No man would want to be seen with me. Ladies would mock me. Oh, I should have departed London weeks ago, and retired in the country."

"Vel," he said, drawing out her name.

Everod was concerned about her. Lady Silver was, too, otherwise she would not have sent him a note asking him to call on the young lady. It was not difficult to guess that the source of her melancholy was her absent lover.

"Perhaps you should cast your pride aside and

summon the babe's father. If he is not aware of your delicate condition, then you should tell him. It is unfair—"

Velouette's dark eyes gave him a scathing look. "Do not speak of unfairness to me, when even from here I have heard rumors of your mischief with a certain young lady. Though beautiful to admire, and an enthusiastic lover, you, Everod, can be a cold, soulless bastard when it comes to getting what you want from others."

Everod frowned at his hat clasped in his hands. "Does this mean you will not marry me, Vel?"

He spoke so matter-of-a-factly that Velouette burst into laughter. Their natures were too alike for them to have a comfortable marriage. The young widow held her stomach as her entire body shook with her glee.

"You wound me, my lady," he said, pleased he had chased away her sadness, even for a few minutes.

Velouette mopped her eyes with her handkerchief. "Nothing wounds you, Ever*hard*," she said, shaking her head at the absurdity. "You would destroy anyone who tried."

The countess's observation bothered him more than it should have. Coming to a decision, he said to her, "Change your dress. I feel like a ride in the park." His fingers brushed hers, and he felt the thump of the baby's kick. Poor Velouette. He would be miserable, too, if he had some cantankerous imp kicking his bowels all day. "I see your son agrees."

Velouette clasped his hand, her gratitude showing in her face. "You are so good to me. I wish you were my son's father."

Everod smiled faintly, but wisely kept his tongue firmly clamped between his teeth.

M iss Keighly, you must think we are terribly forward for arriving at your door in this manner," Kilby Carlisle, Duchess of Solitea, said apologetically after she had introduced Maura to her companions, Lady Fayre and Lady Ramscar.

"Not at all," Maura said, encouraging them all to sit. "I am, however, a little confused by the message you had delivered to the butler. You told Abbot that it was imperative that you see me."

Her Grace glanced at her sister-in-law, Lady Fayre. The other lady nodded encouragingly. "Yes, I did."

All three ladies exhibited varying degrees of discomfort. Maura gingerly sat on the edge of one of the chairs. She had a horrible feeling the trio had not come to offer her friendship.

"You are not here because my aunt spoke to one of your relatives, are you? I thought my aunt Georgette might be meddling again, or even Rowan, uh, Mr. Lidsaw. It is far worse, I suppose."

The Countess of Ramscar possessed a strange sense of humor. She seemed to choke on a bubble of laughter when Maura had mentioned her suspicions about meddling family members. The elegant blonde quickly sobered. Her eyes were kind when she replied, "My apologies, Miss Keighly. I can think of very few things worse than interfering relatives."

"Second only to noisy strangers in your drawing room," Lady Fayre added.

"Still, you are correct," the duchess said, her mouth

pressed tightly, revealing her anger. "What news we bring is as unpleasant to say as it is to deliver."

Maura's gaze drifted from face to face. "Forgive my impertinence, but have I met any of you before? Do you know the Worringtons? My parents, Lord and Lady Courtwill?"

"Our husbands are good friends of someone— well, Lord Everod," Her Grace said bluntly.

The unexpected visit from the trio suddenly made sense. "Oh."

"With the exception of my husband, Mr. Brawley," Lady Fayre said, pretending there hadn't been a sudden lapse in conversation. "My brother, Solitea, Ramscar, Cadd, who is Lord Byrchmore, and of course, Everod, are the gentlemen the *ton* calls *les sauvages nobles*."

"I have heard the nickname, and was aware of Lord Everod's connection," Maura said dully, staring at the silver and pearl ring on her hand. "If you are acquainted with the viscount, then you are also aware of the family discord."

"Your aunt seduced him, and his father did his best to murder him," Lady Ramscar interjected. "It is a family tragedy worthy of the stage."

"And Everod would likely throttle you if he ever glimpsed his life at Covent Garden, Patience," Lady Fayre warned.

Maura pursed her lips, feeling as if she only knew parts of the tale. All three of them seemed very nice, but their connection to Worrington's son created a problem. "I doubt that Lord Everod would be pleased if he learned that you, as his friends, were consorting with his family, even if your intentions to warn me to stay away from the viscount were honorable." She stood. Abbot could see the trio to the door. "Believe it or not, I understand your desire to protect him."

The duchess also stood. With an affection Maura did not deserve, Her Grace grasped both of Maura's hands. "Protect Everod? No, Miss Keighly, we come here to protect you!"

CHAPTER 14

Protect me from Lord Everod?" Maura mused aloud. The duchess's revelation was so unexpected, so generous, she had to blink away the abrupt hint of tears. What did these ladies know that she did not that warranted protection against the viscount? "Your Grace—"

"Kilby," the young woman corrected. "My friends call me by my Christian name. Besides, I think of Fayne and Fayre's mother as the real duchess. I haven't quite grown accustomed to the title."

"Mama would disagree," Lady Fayre argued, moving to stand beside her sister-in-law. "She tells everyone that you rule my brother with a subtle cunning that highly amuses her." She shifted to address Maura. "My brother, Tem, as Mama and I call him, is so smitten with Kilby that he rarely notices when he has been outwitted."

Feeling left out, since she was the only one sitting, the countess rose from the sofa to join them. "You may call me Patience. My husband tells me often that my name does not suit my temperament. May we address you informally? Maura, is it not? It is a pretty name. I believe it means 'dark' in Latin."

"Does it?" Maura replied, feeling a little over-whelmed by the attention of her three guests.

From somewhere beyond the closed door of the drawing room, she heard her aunt calling her name. Maura cast a nervous glance in that direction. "You have to leave." She released the duchess's hands, and stepped back. "Oh, bother, that sounded rude. Ladies, while I appreciate the reasons that brought you here, you all have to go. Now. Aunt Georgette will be upset if she learns that you are friends of Everod's."

Lady Fayre was unimpressed. "Everod has many friends in town. Friends who will defend to the death the honor his own family believes he lacks. If your aunt is concerned about her nerves, perhaps she should remain in the country."

"Maura."

Maura winced. Her aunt had found the butler, and he was telling her about their guests. "If you want to discuss Lord Everod, it will have to be elsewhere," she hissed. "Please!"

The door swung open, and Aunt Georgette walked into the room. She eyed the three young women with a critical, lofty stare that she reserved for individuals that she wanted to intimidate.

"Abbot told me that you had guests."

Although young, her new friends seemed unruffled by her aunt's appearance. Maura quickly made the proper introductions, as she thought of a convincing excuse to bid the ladies farewell.

Her Grace—Kilby—took matters into her own hands. "Lady Worrington, I hope you will not mind if we kidnap your niece for a few hours. The temperate weather has inspired us to visit Hyde Park. If you approve, we would be thrilled to have Miss Keighly join us."

"Of course," her aunt said, the lines around her mouth fading as she relaxed. "The plans we have arranged for the afternoon can be put aside. A little fresh air and friends to share the afternoon with is a pleasant alternative."

Maura tried not to stare openmouthed at her aunt. Lady Fayre had been correct when she had praised what she referred to as Kilby's "subtle cunning" when dealing with her husband. The duchess had appealed to her aunt in a deferring manner that banished any threat Aunt Georgette might have perceived from a lady who was younger, prettier, and outranked her in title.

Lady Fayre noticed Maura's amazement and gave her a conspiring wink.

Maura smiled.

Everod had some fascinating friends.

"Where is Maura?"

Georgette smiled contritely at Rowan. He had arrived earlier to tell her of his late-night encounter with her niece. It boded well that he had managed to kiss Maura, and the young lady, according to her stepson, had welcomed his passionate overture. Encouraged, she had sought out Maura so Rowan could continue his courtship.

The three ladies who had called on her niece were most unexpected. Maura could do worse than befriend a duchess, the daughter of a duke, and a countess.

Georgette had been introduced to the dowager Duchess of Solitea. At least a decade older, and regrettably, merely tolerable in looks, the dowager duchess possessed many friends, Georgette conceded, and considerable influence with the *ton*. Maura could benefit by connecting herself with the family. It was a pity the lady's son was already married, otherwise Georgette might have discarded her plans for Rowan and focused her attentions on securing the duke for her niece.

"I regret Maura has departed with some new friends," Georgette said, placing her hands on his shoulders as she circled behind him. "It appears our girl has found respectable companions all by herself. Her Grace, the Duchess of Solitea, is most gracious to take Maura under her wing. I might add that you could benefit from their friendship, as well."

Rowan halted her gentle massage by squeezing her fingers. "The Duchess of Solitea? Who else? Give me their names," he said tersely.

Annoyed by his callous rejection, she continued her walk around the table that had been brought out onto the terrace. "Two others. The duchess's sister-in-law, Lady Fayre, and a blonde . . . Lady Ramscar, I believe."

Swearing, Rowan slammed down the paper he had been reading before she had returned, and pushed himself onto his feet. "Georgette, these ladies know Everod."

"Gracious, all three were once his mistress?" Georgette exclaimed, impressed with the viscount's appetites. If Worrington had not caught them together, she might have enjoyed Everod for months.

"They were not his lovers, though I am positive their husbands had something to do with my brother's restraint," Rowan said petulantly, a painful reminder of his young age. "Solitea and Ramscar are Everod's friends. The notion that you just sent Maura off with the wives of *les sauvages nobles* gives me to ponder the wisdom of your decision."

Her expression serene, Georgette gracefully sat down in the chair across from Rowan, pretending his revelation had not shaken her to the core. She was a woman who rarely made mistakes. Why had Everod sent his friends' wives to befriend Maura? It frustrated her that she could not seem to anticipate the viscount's moves as he toyed with Worrington and the rest of them.

Eventually, it might become prudent to confront Everod directly. However, she was willing to allow Rowan to be her spy.

She picked up the teapot out of habit, and poured some tea into her cup. "Rowan, my darling man, you look as if you could benefit by taking a brisk ride in the park."

Rowan nodded, grimly satisfied with her plan. "I see."

Georgette clasped her hands together and tucked them under her chin. "I never told Maura that you were here. If she encounters you at the park, she will think it simply a coincidence."

No harm had been done by her misstep. If the Duchess of Solitea and her friends had approached Maura for something other than friendship, Rowan would alert her.

Georgette had no intention of giving Everod the chance to outwit her.

S hall we walk from here?" the young duchess, Kilby, solicitously inquired. "We could take the footpath to the river. The view is magnificent."

"The scenery is a favorite for artists from the Royal Academy. You will often encounter them sitting along the grassy banks with an easel erected beside them; a pencil clenched between their teeth and another poised in their hand," Lady Fayre added to further entice her.

"A walk sounds wonderful," Maura said enthusiastically.

Kilby commanded the coachman to halt.

While the duchess issued orders to her servant, Maura leaned forward anticipating their upcoming adventure. Aunt Georgette's timely interruption had given her an excuse to escape the confines of the house. Perhaps it was not ladylike to admit it, but Maura was used to exploring the family lands on foot. Since her arrival in London, all her outings seemed to require a carriage.

This time of day, the park was as busy as Bond Street. Horses and equipages of varying sizes rumbled by them as the ladies descended their carriage with the assistance of a groom. Pedestrians were everywhere, enjoying the scenery as well as being seen. Colorful blankets were scattered across the open field like spring petals, as couples and families appreciated the fine weather. Two young boys dashed in front of Maura, halting her stride, while a third boy, the pursuer, chased after his faster companions.

If Maura had been younger, she might have joined the boys in their merriment.

The coachman remained beside the horses while the groom followed the four ladies at a leisurely pace.

"How long have you known Lord Everod?" Maura asked her companions, admiring the varied landscape of woods, hills, and meadow.

Fayre was the first to respond to her question. "My brother, Tem, and Everod have been friends since they were boys. I cannot recall a year when Everod was not at my brother's side. He often visited Arion-rod when I was a girl. I was suitably impressed with my brother's friend."

Fayre opened her parasol, a frilly thing with tiny red bows at the edge. Maura also opened her parasol. Hers was made from white lace with white tassels dangling from fixed points.

"Even then, Everod was taller than my brother," Fayre revealed, as she walked beside Maura. "In my young mind, taller meant he could throttle my brother. For that alone, I was smitten for a summer."

All four ladies laughed, imaging the child with long cinnamon braids chasing after Everod with the hope that he might kill her brother at her whim.

Maura glanced away uncomfortably, realizing she had also pursued young Everod. She had been older than Fayre, but she had been smitten with his arrogant smirk and playful ways. Unlike Fayre, Maura feared she had never quite outgrown her youthful fascination for the man.

"Of course, I was beneath both my brother's and Everod's notice. I was merely the annoying younger sister," she explained to them. "It was just as well. The few occasions I did manage to coax my brother into allowing me to partake in one of their adventures were a complete disaster. They always brought me home crying, my dress soiled and torn, and bloodied welts on my face and arms."

"How dreadful!" Patience said.

Kilby and Patience were to Maura's right. Still smiling at Fayre's tale, she said to them, "Have you both known Lord Everod as long?"

"Patience's husband, Ram, has known Everod as long as Fayne, I suppose," Kilby replied, glancing at her friend for confirmation. "I met Everod two years ago, when circumstances placed me directly in Fayne's path."

"You were fortunate Tem saw you first," Fayre teased. "Otherwise, Everod might have vied for your attentions."

Patience giggled. "I concur. I have known Everod for thirteen months, and according to my husband, the viscount tends to flirt outrageously with anything wearing a skirt. I confess, there is something about Everod that sends a lady's heart racing—"

"Or has a lady pondering what it might feel like to have his hot lips on hers. Are his kisses as potent as strong brandy?" Fayre wondered aloud with a wistful sigh.

Maura opened her mouth, almost falling into the trap of acknowledging that she knew exactly how Everod's kisses affect a lady. The viscount's kisses were potent. If she closed her eyes, she could still feel his hot breath on her face as his mouth slanted over hers. He tasted heavenly, too. An intelligent lady could dedicate hours to kissing the man, analyzing every detail.

Maura swallowed before she embarrassed herself by drooling. She must have had an odd expression on her face, because all three ladies were staring at her peculiarly.

"We're too late. The scoundrel has already kissed you, hasn't he?" Kilby said shrewdly. "Or worse."

Maura halted, feeling that her new friends had neatly maneuvered her into a corner. "I—"

Fayre surprised her by placing her arm around her waist, her eyes brimming with compassion. "Do not bother denying it. Kilby overheard Everod's admission to my brother that he hoped to do more than kiss you."

"We love Everod dearly, Maura," Kilby said as she and Patience circled around her. "However, the man is a scoundrel. During the two years of our acquaintance, he has discarded so many mistresses that I have lost count."

Patience nodded in agreement. "Your connection to his family makes you vulnerable. It is not our place to interfere—"

Fayre finished the countess's thought. "However, you are different from his usual lovers."

"I am *not* his lover," Maura denied swiftly.

"Not yet," Kilby replied, placing her hand on Maura's arm. "Everod usually chooses companions who understand his nature. He is a faithless, flirtatious selfish beast. Widows and courtesans are his normal fare. These ladies do not presume they can cage him, nor would he permit it if they tried."

"Seducing virgins for sport or revenge sounds too unsavory, even for Everod," Fayre said, confident that she understood the viscount's character. "I do not presume to comprehend what is going on between you and Everod, but we could not in good conscience allow him to ruin an innocent woman for spite."

Maura lowered her parasol, collapsing it as the point touched the gravel path. Fayre's concerns distressed Maura. Her heart silently cried out in denial, rejecting the vile portrait of Everod's character. She had not wanted to believe Everod could hurt her, but these three ladies, who knew him better than she, thought he was not only capable, but plotting her ruination.

"Good afternoon, ladies," Everod said, startling all four of them from their private musings. He was not alone. A beautiful, very pregnant lady had her hand on his arm as he strode up to them. "Have I arrived in time or have you three filled Maura's head with tales of my savagery?"

His forbidding amber-green eyes moved from face to face, and his displeasure sullied the air around them like a menacing fog.

"Really, Everod," the exotic dark-haired lady at his side said, laughing. "Most ladies, present company excluded naturally, find your rough, impulsive nature appealing."

"We would not presume to delay you or your friend, Lord Everod," Kilby said, unruffled that she and her companions had just been caught doing exactly what Everod had suspected. "Enjoy your walk."

Everod was staring directly at Maura, silently daring her to accuse him of some dastardly deed.

"Come along, ladies," Fayre said, giving Maura a shove when she did not respond.

The four of them hurried down the footpath without glancing back to see if the incensed viscount was charging after them.

S he is very pretty," Velouette observed, staring at the departing ladies. "Innocent, too. It clings to some ladies like a floral scent."

"What are you implying, Vel?" Everod snarled, half tempted to run after Maura and demand that she tell him everything his friends's wives had told her about him. "Do you think I am too jaded for Miss Keighly?"

Women. Without hearing his side of things, they had circled around Maura, attempting to protect her from his vile intentions. He wondered if Solitea and Ram knew what mischief their wives had engaged in this afternoon when they called on Maura. The trio deserved a sore backside for interfering in his life.

"Darling, you are too jaded for most ladies," she said, patting him on the cheek. "Still, it does not prevent us from slowing our stride so you are able to catch us."

N o one deigned to speak again until they stood on the banks of the Serpentine River, which seemed more like a lake that was fed by a small stream since its perimeter reminded Maura of a parallelogram. Rowboats and small sailboats glided across the mirrored surface alongside ducks and swans. Kilby had been

correct. It was a picturesque spot to pause, and appreciate the beauty around them. As Fayre had predicted,
several artists were arduously immortalizing what they
saw to paper using watercolors and charcoal.

"Who was the lady with Lord Everod?" Maura
asked, giving in to her curiosity.

"Lady Spryng," Fayre said, reluctant to say more.

Maura refused to suppress the obvious question
burning on her tongue. "His mistress?"

"Lady Spryng has been every man's mistress,"
Kilby spat, her dislike for the pregnant lady transpar-
ent to anyone who noted her expression. "Or has tried
to be."

The duchess squeezed her eyes shut, striving to remain calm. "Forgive me, Maura, I do not mean to
sound unkind. However, there are some ladies of the
ton who have no qualms about stealing another lady's
husband. Lady Spryng and her ilk are best when
avoided."

Maura glanced sideways at Fayre, who subtly shook
her head in warning. Obviously, Kilby had a good reason to dislike the exotic beauty.

"Is Lord Everod the sire of Lady Spryng's child?"
Maura held her breath awaiting a reply to her question.

Patience's forehead furrowed. "I highly doubt it.
Lord Everod might be a scoundrel, but he is rather possessive about things that he considers his. If Lady
Spryng carried Everod's child, he would have claimed
the babe, and I have not heard any rumors that he has
done so. I believe he and Lady Spryng are just friends."

"Knowing Everod, she is for certain a former mistress," Fayre said, disillusioning Maura with her news. "She is too beautiful, and there have been rumors about *her*."

Maura grudgingly thought Everod and Lady Spryng seemed perfect for each other. His tall, brooding, handsome features complemented Lady Spryng's smooth light brown skin, sleek sable hair, and dark, inviting eyes. Everod would not have bothered to resist her considerable charms. Perhaps the lady's position was not that of former mistress as her companions assumed.

It was a disparaging thought.

On horseback, Rowan Lidsaw had discreetly observed Maura's encounter with his elder brother. Whatever the ladies' motives for befriending Maura, even from his considerable distance he could see that the three women had been displeased with Everod when he approached them.

Georgette would be as delighted as he was that their exchange was brief. Maura and her new friends had continued down the footpath to the river, while Everod and his pregnant companion had strolled toward their awaiting carriage.

Was the lady carrying Everod's bastard?

The complication of his brother's carelessness could benefit Rowan. Maura was too innocent to fathom the dark nature of a man's lust. She was likely appalled when she saw Everod promenading his whore so publicly in the park. The woman's ruination was a cruel example of what Maura would perceive as Everod's weakness, and she would shun him out of respect for the poor woman carrying his child.

The Duchess of Solitea and her friends had been allies after all.

Pleased, Rowan dug his heels into the gelding's hindquarters, already anticipating Georgette's joy when he shared his good news with her.

CHAPTER 15

Georgette had greeted Maura warmly upon her return from Hyde Park with her new friends. While her aunt spoke of the advantages for being connected with the eccentric Carlisles, Maura pondered their brief encounter with Everod.

He had been as surprised as she had been to see him. Nor had he been ashamed to be caught with his mistress or former mistress. No, Everod had been furious with Kilby, Fayre, and Patience for their interference. Everod believed the ladies could damage Maura's fine opinion of him, and he had barely restrained himself from throttling her friends.

Lady Spryng, on the other hand, seemed rather amused by his reaction. Maura had felt the weight of the other woman's measured stare. She had known exactly who Maura was, and likely her part in Everod's downfall twelve years ago. Instead of condemning Maura, Lady Spryng had teased Everod into a guarded retreat. Whoever this woman was to the viscount, she carried a certain amount of influence with him.

It was only later that Maura realized that she had not spoken a single word during the odd encounter with Everod. Of course, if she had managed to utter something clever, what could she have said? Kilby, Patience, and Fayre had done their best to prepare her for any deception from Everod. Her aunt, uncle, and Rowan also believed Everod was dangerous.

Everod in his own swaggering manner had also warned her off.

She held up her hand and stared at the ornate pearl and silver ring on her finger. Everod had secretly given her trinkets that belonged to his mother. Should she listen to his words, and the words of others, or judge the viscount by his actions?

Everod had expected, nay, dared her to condemn him at the park. He was a man who liked to gamble and play games. Was he wagering that Maura might possess the cunning to glimpse the man beneath the polished, sarcastic mask that he presented to the world or was it all a ruse to strike at the family?

The questions circled around in Maura's brain all evening. Fortunately, she and Georgette had attended a music performance which concealed her inattentiveness. She barely listened to the opera singer, though her aunt had praised the lady's voice.

Worrington had not joined them. He had become ill while visiting one of his clubs. Abbot had told her privately that the earl had collapsed in the front hall, though her uncle kept insisting that he was just tired. Concerned about her husband, Georgette was prepared to cancel their evening out, but Worrington insisted that they attend the musical recital without him.

With her aunt worrying about the earl, and Maura distracted about Everod, both women were relieved when the evening ended.

Georgette kissed Maura on the cheek. Moving to the stairs, she said, "Forgive me, little one, for not being a better companion this evening."

"I understand, Aunt," Maura said softly, joining her aunt at the base of the staircase. "Give Uncle a kiss from me. I pray that he has recovered his strength."

"I will." Georgette embraced Maura. "I think we both forget that Worrington is not a young man. He is seven and sixty, and though he will not admit it aloud, he suffers from many ills related to his old age." The countess tapped her first finger against her forehead. "However, if I have anything to say on the matter, Worrington will live another sixty years. I have several treatises on potent herbs in my bedchamber. What Worrington needs is one of my restoratives!"

Maura grinned at her aunt's enthusiasm. Like her sister, Georgette had been born a scientist, though the lady would deny that she possessed the intellect or ambition. "I love you, Aunt Georgette. I have no doubt that Worrington will improve under your care."

Her aunt hooked her arm through Maura's as they climbed the stairs together. "You know me, my treasured girl. I can be most determined when I want something."

Maura awoke to the low rumble of thunder in the distance. Or so she thought. The sound could have been part of her tumultuous dreams. Sitting up, she tilted her head and listened. Everything was quiet. Perhaps she had been dreaming, after all.

She pushed back the blankets and slid out of bed. Going to the window, she leaned against the stubborn sash until her window opened. She stuck her head through the opening and inhaled. The air was humid. The wind picked up, smelling ripe with the scent of the approaching storm.

Maura smiled when she saw a flash of lightning. Thunder followed seconds later.

While some people cowered in fear at the thought of a violent storm, Maura loved them. The wind caught her hair, lifting the dark strands in front of her face and making them dance. She did not know how long she had been sleeping, but the hour mattered little to her. Retreating back into her bedchamber, Maura searched the floor for her slippers. Another blind search in her wardrobe produced a hooded cloak of dark blue made of fine wool with an inner lining of gold silk. The garment was a bit extravagant for a walk in the gardens to watch the approaching storm, but it offered her some modest protection.

The dark cloak also covered her nightgown, allowing her to blend with the night. Like a ghost she slowly made her way downstairs, and slipped into the back gardens through the conservatory. She had not bothered lighting a candle or fussing with a lantern. Maura knew the layout of the house and gardens, and the occasional flash of lightning guided her when she hesitated.

Stepping outdoors, she spun around and savored the feel of the air on her face. The wind caressed her like phantom fingers coaxing her to play. A flicker of lightning whitened the midnight sky overhead, revealing a gazebo to her left. Her gait was unhurried as she made her way to the wooden structure. From there, she could watch the storm and spare her pretty cloak from the rain.

The first drops of rain struck her face when she was halfway between the house and gazebo. Pulling the hood of the cloak up, Maura pinched the ends together at her chin so the wind did not catch the fabric. Several yards later, the heavens opened and the sudden downpour was as blinding as the darkness.

"Oh, very wise of you, Maura Keighly," she muttered, reaching out with her right hand so she did not run headlong into the gazebo. "A late-night walk in the gardens with lightning singeing the heavens. Just to watch a silly storm. Your aunt will think you are daft, my girl!"

She stumbled as her foot connected with the first wooden step. With her rain-soaked cloak tangling her limbs, Maura pitched forward, her knees and elbows taking the brunt of her fall.

Maura groaned. She crawled up the remaining three steps before she sat down. Gingerly, she touched her left elbow. "If I broke a bone, I will never hear the end of it."

"I grant you, it was not the most graceful arrival I have witnessed," Everod mused aloud, causing her to whirl around and shriek. "Fortunately, I am a charitable gent."

The viscount was just a disembodied voice until the quick flash of lightning revealed him. He was leaning against the railing just to the right of her, bareheaded, his black hair glistening from the rain. If he grinned at her humiliating predicament, Maura intended to murder him.

"You are a brave lady, Maura Keighly," he said, extending his hand to her. "Just how brave remains to be seen. Come to me, pretty Maura. If you do, I will tenderly kiss your wounds and vanquish all your hurts."

While Everod had entertained a rather delicious fantasy of Maura coming to him in the night, he never expected the lady to be so obliging. Especially after Kilby, Fayre, and Patience's noble attempt to warn Maura off. He had been flabbergasted to see the four women walking together at the park. Another gent might have been flattered that his friends' wives had taken such an interest in his liaisons.

He wasn't amused.

When his sluggish brain began working again, he could only guess that Kilby had overheard part of his conversation with Solitea.

Christ, a man had no privacy once he married. The next time he visited his friend, he would personally lock the nosy duchess in her bedchamber to keep her from interfering in his life.

Maura winced as she stood. Apparently disgusted and a little embarrassed, she thrust back her hood. She looked magnificent. Her pale creamy skin glowed even after the lightning had faded. The hood had not spared her long curling tresses from the rain. The hair framing her oval face was damp, and dangled like black strings. Maura wiped away the strands of hair sticking to her cheeks.

Noticing that he had shifted his stance, she held out her hand. "Stay where you are, my lord. No one has kissed my skinned knee since I was . . ." She glanced down at her hands, her eyelashes fanned over her cheeks like obsidian spikes.

As he crossed his arms, her abrupt silence prompted a forgotten memory to surface. "Since you were ten," he said, and her head snapped up in surprise. "I had taunted you into climbing one of the large oaks. You were too mad at me to worry about reaching the lowest hanging branch. However, you panicked when you tried to climb down. You took half the bark off that old tree before your bottom smacked the ground."

"Good grief, the tree was fine! I, on the other hand, got nasty scrapes down the front of both legs and the inside of my left arm while I tried not to break my neck." A hint of a smile shimmered on her face, but she was too annoyed with him to reveal it. "You were laughing so hard, you were of little help."

"You insult me, Maura," Everod said, edging closer. "I was quite chivalrous for my young age. While you sat beneath the tree sniveling—"

"I was not sniveling!"

The girl had been sniveling. Most little girls were champion snivelers. It seemed rude to disagree so he refrained from repeating his observation. "I raced to the stream and moistened my handkerchief. It was I who washed the worst of your scrapes and—"

"Kissed both my knees." Her bare arms slipped from the confines of her cloak as she pointed to a spot near her left elbow. "And here." She gave him a sad, enigmatic smile. "You were my hero that day."

It was likely the last day Maura had deemed him heroic. Weeks later, he had succumbed to his curiosity and Georgette's wiles, and his life had taken its devilish course. Not that Everod was the type to complain about his life. His banishment had not been filled with strife. Worrington would have never permitted his heir to perish from the elements or starvation. Through his solicitor, Everod had received an allowance for his living expenses. There had been only one stipulation. Everod was to stay away from his family.

It had been a fair deal.

Besides, Everod had been too angry to desire reconciliation with his beloved family.

"Why are you here?" Maura demanded, some of her former spirit returning now that her fear and embarrassment had eased.

Everod suspected that his answer would only frighten her again. Instead, he asked, "Why are you not in bed?"

Maura gestured awkwardly at the blowing sheets of rain that separated her from the safety of the house. "I was. I awoke to the sound of thunder."

"Ah . . . you fear storms," he said, feeling indulgent at what he viewed as a feminine weakness. Since he was sharing the shelter of the gazebo with her, he would happily offer her a protective arm and shoulder to rest her cheek upon.

"Of course, not!" she said scathingly, causing him to blink at her temper. "I love storms. This particular one sounded miles and miles away. The air was so warm and sweet, I thought I might sit and watch the storm as it blew in." She gave him a chagrined glance. "The storm won the foot race."

His affection for thunderstorms was growing. "How providential I was available to keep you company until the storm passed."

"And why is that, Everod?" Maura asked, returning him to the question he had neatly avoided in the first round. "Skulking around Worrington's garden must be low on your list of evening amusements."

Maura could be quite sarcastic when she chose to be. Since he had been accused countless times of the same bad habit, he found it rather endearing.

"What if I told you that I knew of your habit of walking the gardens when sleep escaped you," he said, approaching her so she was forced to back against one of the railings.

"Oh."

"I suffer from insomnia on occasion," he confessed, the corner of his mouth quirking when her expressive eyes widened. "Is it so far-fetched that I might seek out a fellow sufferer, and perhaps share the night with her?"

Maura nibbled her lip as she contemplated his explanation. "Yes!" She shoved at his chest, and moved away from him.

Everod was content to let her go. After all, the storm raged around them, and her only shelter was the gazebo.

"You are lying." She whirled around and pointed an accusing finger at him. "You want to know the details of my conversation with Kilby, Fayre, and Patience."

"Already chums, and calling one another by your first names," he muttered, marveling at how quickly ladies could bond in friendship, particularly when a man was involved. He parted his hands in surrender. "You're correct. I was lying. I am curious about your outing, and more to the point, what was said."

A wind gust caused Maura to shiver. Her cloak was damp, and it was chilling her even though the air was warm. She reached for the clasp, but hesitated, shooting him a disgruntled look.

"Your cloak is soaked, and you are clearly uncomfortable," he said reasonably. "With the exception of the occasional flash of lightning, your modesty is safe."

"I was not expecting gentlemen callers so late," Maura said crisply. "I wear only my nightgown underneath my cloak."

"Sweet Maura, I swear I have glimpsed countless nightgowns," he said, deliberately adding a patronizing tone to his voice. "I doubt you will shock me by revealing yours."

Everod grinned in the darkness. The air around them heated as her ire with him increased. "Perhaps. However, I will kindly pass on your arrogant invitation for me to show you mine!"

He crossed the distance between them swiftly. Before she could protest, he unfastened the clasp at her throat. The sodden cloak plopped in a heap.

"How dare you!" she fumed, raising her hands like claws as if she were planning to throttle him.

Everod seized her wrists. Lightning flickered violently and the echoing thunder shook their humble shelter. As she struggled to free herself from his grip, he noticed the twinkle of silver on her hand. Intrigued, he dragged her against his unyielding body, so he could study the trinket on her finger.

"Let me go!"

"What is this?" he said, hinting that he had made a monumental discovery. He already recognized the piece. The next bout of lightning confirmed his suspicions.

Maura wore his mother's ring.

Mayhap, his fears about what Kilby and the other ladies had said to Maura were unfounded.

"You are wearing my ring," he said, bracing his hands on the railing on each side of her, effectively caging her with his body.

"Your mother's ring," Maura countered, attempting to diminish the significance of her decision.

"Same thing, since I gave you my mother's treasures."

The white nightgown Maura wore to bed was so thin it floated around her calves like dandelion seeds on a spring breeze. His right hand on the railing tightened into a fist. His longing to touch her was ruining his good intentions to handle Maura gently.

Maura stared at his chest. Earlier, he had removed his coat and waistcoat due to the humid quality in the air. He had also untied his cravat, allowing the ends to hang loosely around his neck.

"Forgive me for not thanking you properly for returning the necklace and giving me the rest of the matching pieces." Maura cleared her throat, and seemed to brace herself before raising her lashes to look him directly in the eyes. "I would have, had there been a proper moment."

A moment when neither his friends nor family were observing them.

What they shared was private. Everod was growing tired of everyone standing in his way from what he wanted. He was a man who rarely hesitated in laying claim to what he considered his.

Maura was too innocent to understand the temptation she represented for him. Too trusting. He was ruthless enough to exploit her weakness for his benefit, and possessed enough recklessness to risk his life for a taste of her unguarded passion.

"Here's your chance to show your gratitude," Everod said, shuffling his feet closer so her soft breasts pressed into his chest. "A quiet moment with no one watching while you thank me properly."

Maura peered at him. She did not trust him. "You have my thanks, my lord."

"And?" he prompted, content to hold her body against his the rest of the night.

She shook her head in confusion, searching his shadowed face for some clue. "A kiss?"

"It's a start," he murmured, tipping her chin up so he could claim his prize.

CHAPTER 16

Listening to the rain as it battered the roof of the gazebo, Maura closed her eyes, surrendering to Everod's kiss. Like the storm that had lured her outdoors, his mouth caressed her with the lightest touch. The sensation spun her around like a whirlwind, making her dizzy and giddy that she was experiencing something unfettered and forbidden to her.

Maura leaned up on her toes, encouraging him to take more. She was unprepared for his response. Crushing her back into the railing behind her, Everod threaded his fingers into her long hair and devoured her with his mouth. The gentle kiss that she had savored became almost punishing in its intensity. He nipped her lower lip sharply, and pushed his tongue past her teeth, capturing her tongue with his.

He was overwhelming her.

A low sound of protest vibrated in her throat. He ignored it. Her lips felt bruised as he kneaded the tender flesh under his rough demands. Breathless, she clutched his arms in an attempt to push him away. He seemed encouraged by her actions. Panic rose in her belly when Maura felt the viscount's hand close over her breast.

She tore her mouth away from his. "No! No! No!"

Maura shoved at him until he released her. No longer caring if she was drenched by the rain, Maura ran into the night.

"Maura!"

The downpour muffled his shout, spurring her to hasten her pace. Everod caught her only yards away from the gazebo. Belatedly, she realized that she had never stood a chance in escaping him. He always had the advantage.

Both of them were soaked to the skin. The storm she had come to watch no longer seemed friendly. She flinched at the next clap of thunder.

"Are you crazy?" Everod roared into her face.

She pushed her wet hair out of her face, and turned to fight her way back to the house. The late hour guaranteed that no one would see her when she slipped back into the house. If she cleaned up the mess, no one would have to know that she had left her bedchamber at all.

Everod grabbed her arm, determined to drag her back to the gazebo. "We're not finished!" he snarled. When she slipped in the mud, he picked her up and carried her.

"My slipper! I lost it." Maura squinted against the darkness and the rain. A fine misty fog had developed obscuring her vision the ground around them.

"You've lost your mind if you think I'll wallow about in the mud to find it!" he said, putting her down when he had cleared the last step. "Are you cold?"

Maura crossed her arms over her breasts and turned away when she noticed the wet nightgown was

practically sheer. "No." The air was still warm. The
rain felt slightly cooler than her bathwater. "What are
you doing with my cloak?"

Everod's shirt was plastered to his skin. Water
droplets dripped steadily from his queue as if it were
a spout rather than hair. "Spreading it out so we have
something to sit upon," he said without glancing at
her. "My coat is over there. Put it on. It should give
you back the modesty that you think I tried to bribe
from you."

He was being churlish.

That's what she told herself when she stomped
away from him and reached for his coat. Maura
slipped her arms through the long sleeves, feeling silly
in the oversized garment. It also smelled of Everod,
but she tried not to dwell on that aspect. Unsure if he
would accept anything from her, Maura snatched up
his waistcoat.

She walked over to him and held out the garment.
"It will feel better than your shirt, I wager."

Everod gave her a considering look before accepting the waistcoat. While she settled down on top of
the cloak, he turned away and peeled off his soaked
shirt. Tossing it away, he put on the waistcoat. He sat
down beside her without speaking and removed his
shoes and stockings. Maura frowned at the single
slipper on her left foot. It was muddied, and definitely
not helping her return to the house. She kicked it off.

"Should I apologize?" Maura asked, not liking the
silence between them.

"I was thinking as much," was his brusque retort.

Maura was so taken aback by his unexpected response that she started laughing. Holding the edges of his coat together, she rocked back and forth, her eyes full of mirth. Well, Everod could not truly appreciate her expression, but after their scuffle she was feeling rather foolish.

A brutal man who thought only of ravishing the lady within reach would not have rushed into the storm concerned for her welfare. Nor would he have given her his coat because he sensed her discomfort. Everod was no man's image of a saint, but she conceded that she had misjudged his actions.

She tucked her legs under her, covering them as best she could with the coat. "I might have behaved—"

"Like a lunatic?" he smoothly supplied.

"Rashly." Maura leaned against the balusters of the railing circling the gazebo. It lacked comfort, but it eased the cramp in her lower back. "What was I supposed to think, Everod? This afternoon I saw you strolling in the park with your pregnant mistress."

The darkness did not prevent him from pinning her with his infuriated gaze. "Though none of your business, I see I must clarify my connection to Lady Spryng. Though we were once close, our liaison ended years ago. The lady is merely a friend. The babe she carries is not mine."

Kilby and the others had speculated that Lady Spryng would have been unable to resist the virile Lord Everod. He seemed too insulted by her accusation to be lying. "And your mother's jewelry," she said quietly. She held up her hand. The pearls gleamed faintly up at her. "Why did you give me something so precious?"

Maura heard him sigh wearily.

"The ring, bracelets, and earrings have sat in a box for years," he explained, stirring the air with his hand. "I could tell that you loved the necklace. You were loath to return it to me, but you did so anyway because it was the proper thing to do. Though you do not resemble my mother in looks, you do in temperament. If my mother was alive, I know it would please her that you appreciated her treasures as much as she did."

"Oh, Everod."

He shifted, moving closer to her. "My actions are not selfless, Maura. Maybe it pleases me to see you wearing something I gave you."

"Then I would not presume to insult you by offering your gifts back," she said, noticing he had insinuated his arm between the balusters and her back. Once again, he had sensed her unspoken need. Maura leaned against his arm, savoring his firmness and the warmth his body was emitting.

"Since we are being truthful," he murmured, smoothing her hair with his free hand. "There is something else you should know."

Maura tilted her head back. "Pray what, my lord?"

"I have every intention of seducing you."

Maura laughed.

She thought he was jesting, but Everod was always serious when it came to bedding a lady he desired. He recognized the inviting slumberous gaze of a woman ready to be tumbled into his bed. Perhaps Maura was unaware of her own desires, but he had glimpsed that greedy yearning in her sea-gray eyes. When he held her in his arms, she melted against him as if she belonged there.

Everod was battling his own unruly lust for Maura.

Though he had not given her his mother's jewelry to buy her favors, the needs eroding his control might have provoked him to offer Maura anything to gain her consent.

He snickered at his eagerness. If he had any sense, he would carry her back to the house, and let her believe he was jesting. Of course, most of his friends would have claimed he was lacking both scruples and his sanity. Everod hoped Maura would not test the limits of both.

"It wasn't a jest."

Maura sobered immediately. "I have no desire to be your mistress, Everod. From what your friends' wives have told me, there are many ladies of the *ton* who already claim the dubious honor."

His jaw clenched at the reminder of Kilby, Fayre, and Patience's mischief. "I am not asking you to be my mistress."

"Or your wife!"

There was grim amusement in his inflection when he said, "Why, you are a brave lady, Maura Keighly! Are you willing to bind yourself to a faithless scoundrel? A man whose own father cannot look upon him without spewing threats and blame?"

She tried to scoot away from him, but he seized the front of his coat and pulled her close so he could see her face. "I thought not." He relaxed his fingers, releasing the coat. "Besides, I am not offering you marriage. I desire you, Maura. You feel the same. If you deny it, you will force me to call you a liar."

Maura said nothing.

He had probably surprised her with his blunt speech. The lady was used to flowery declarations and sloppy kisses from puppies like his brother, Rowan. If there had been a lamp or a candle, Maura would have seen the burgeoning proof of his desire. Unbeknownst to her, he had been required to adjust his rigid cock several times within his breeches since he had carried her into the gazebo.

All he thought about was freeing himself, and pushing his cock into her.

"It would be wrong," she said finally. "How could I trust you?"

"You are Georgette's niece," he countered coolly. "Why should I trust *you*?"

Logic and lust rarely shared the same portion of the brain. Everod sensed she was straightening, working herself up to give him a hundred reasons why they could not close their eyes to the problems between them and surrender to their mutual attraction.

Everod was not interested in listening to her arguments.

He had not listened to his own internal debates on why he should stay away from Maura Keighly.

If he had, he would not have been skulking about his father's town gardens in the middle of the night.

He would not be on the brink of taking Maura's innocence.

Everod slipped his thumb under the fabric of his coat and slowly pushed it down, exposing one of her arms. "You don't need this any longer." He freed her other arm.

"Everod."

God, how he wished he could see more than beguiling glimpses of her pale features when the lightning obliged him. Was she frightened or resigned? Or maybe she was relieved he was taking the decision out of her hands? "The nightgown must go, too. Let the breeze dry your skin."

Instead of relieving Maura of the garment, Everod waited. After a few minutes, he heard the soft brush of fabric against skin. Seconds later, there was a distinct plop as the wet nightgown struck the wood flooring. Finally remembering to exhale, he removed the waistcoat. He preferred the satin feel of flesh gliding against flesh.

Everod got onto his knees and unfastened his breeches. His hands trembled slightly as he rushed through the necessary task. He was unworried that Maura would change her mind about accepting him as her lover. His haste was due to his growing excitement in bedding her. That fact alone should have given him pause. Standing, he shoved his breeches down and kicked the garment aside, his thoughts directed solely on the woman in front of him.

"Here, lie back," he instructed, using his coat to pillow her head.

"I do not—I do not know how to pleasure you," Maura confessed, her voice quivering as if she had uttered an unforgivable sin.

Her concern for his needs touched his jaded heart. It left him more determined that she would not leave him regretting their lovemaking. He kissed her, nuzzling her lips until she responded. "I am easy to please," he said, trailing his fingers down her throat, between her breasts, to her flat stomach.

Pulling himself up, Everod moved between her legs. "I promised to kiss all your pain away."

"That is unnecessary," she said, gasping as he skimmed the unblemished skin from her knee to the inner thigh and marveled at its softness.

Maura trembled beneath his tender, questing caresses, her body tense. He did not fool himself into believing that it was anticipation of the pleasure that awaited them that had her slender frame as taut as a bow.

He kissed her knee. "I insist." Everod shifted and brought her other knee up, and pressed his lips against her kneecap.

"It barely hurts," she protested, when he moved lower so his lips could nibble her thigh.

"Truly? Then I am not doing this correctly."

He laughed at her muttered oath. At least he thought it was an oath. Then again, he supposed a lady like Maura did not swear. Everod slid his hand higher up her leg until his fingers grazed the soft hair nestled between her legs. Everod petted her hidden cleft, and her body jerked in reaction. Delving deeper, his fingers met no resistance. He groaned as proof of her arousal coated his thumb.

Maura desired this coupling as much as he did.

Since he had espied her standing on Bond Street, conversing with her bitch of an aunt, he had circled, taunted, and teased her senses to bring them both to this moment. Everod had coaxed her body into desiring him, even when her mind and heart were uncertain of his motives. *He* was undecided what he wanted from Maura beyond the mutual release she had been denying them both.

Now was not the time for puzzling out the answers to the unspoken questions whispering in their respective heads. Maura was naked and splayed out upon the cloak like a willing sacrifice. The night and the storm shielded them. No one was awake to stop him, and Everod thought he might die if he did not get inside her.

Without giving her a chance to change her mind, he crawled on top of Maura. His arms took the brunt of his weight as he nudged her legs apart, positioning himself between her thighs. Reaching down, he wrapped his hand around his pulsing cock and squeezed. Each second he hesitated driving himself into her soft beckoning channel was heightening his exquisite agony.

He rubbed the head of his cock against her dewy cleft. "Do not beg me to stop. I am not as honorable as you believe, Maura. I intend to possess all of you this evening."

Maura touched his cheek. "I know."

Using his fingers to guide the head of his cock, Everod pressed deeper into her cleft, seeking the liquid, welcoming heat of her feminine sheath. Despite the mild temperature, and gusting wind wafting through the open structure, sweat was dampening his brow as he sank deeper into Maura only to meet the fragile resistance of her innocence.

Maura stiffened at the slight pain of his invasion.

A virgin.

Everod had always known she was untouched. Before Maura, he had avoided bedding virgins. He was not squeamish about deflowering an innocent. Regrettably, the lingering consequences generally outweighed the little pleasure he might gain from the experience. Marriage-minded matrons were also a nuisance. None of these arguments seemed to deter him from sparing Maura the initial pain his penetration would cause her.

Glaring down at her, angry at himself for not being the patient lover a woman like Maura romanticized about, he said harshly, "Your innocence won't change anything. It's mine to take, just as your body was meant to be mine."

To prove it, Everod pushed his cock deeper into her tight channel. Maura closed her eyes, her fingernails digging into his forearms to eloquently express the pain he was causing her.

"It hurts," she whispered.

He was not a selfish lover. Nor was he insensitive to her discomfort. This was one of the reasons why he had not troubled himself with virgins. He had erroneously believed that a slow penetration would be kinder to her sensitive flesh.

"I've changed my mind." He eased out of her.

"What?"

He heard the surprise in her voice. Without warning, Everod plunged sharply into her sheath, piercing the barrier that prevented him from entering her wholly. They both cried out; hers was of pain, his was of triumph.

Everod braced his forehead on her shoulder and shut his eyes. Maura's sheath constricted his cock like a second skin. He held himself still, allowing her to become accustomed to his invasion.

"We've done it, Maura. I'm inside you," he said, gliding his right hand over her buttock and hauling her firmly against his pelvis. "Am I hurting you?"

"If I say 'yes' . . . will you kiss me and vanquish all my hurts?" She wiggled her spine, a small shifting movement to accommodate his weight and the rigid part of him that was buried so fully into her moist, spicy core.

"Cheeky wench," he said affectionately. "Only you would dare to tease me at such a time."

"Would you prefer that I succumb to a maidenly bout of vapors?"

Everod nipped her chin with his teeth. "And miss all the fun? Never."

It took amazing strength not to move within her. To distract her, his hand closed around her breast. He teased her swollen nipples, circling his thumb over the sensitive flesh until she unconsciously arched against him.

"That's it," he crooned, nudging his hip against hers. The delicious friction of the small movement almost sent him over the edge. "My brave girl, it's time to vanquish both our pain."

Everod withdrew, and thrust completely into her snug quim. There was no resistance from her body.

Her sheath yielded to his uncompromising strokes. Maura initially lay passively beneath him, accepting his claiming as he rubbed his body against hers. As she grew accustomed to his steady rhythm, she became bolder. Increasingly her hips rose to meet his, coaxing him to greater depths.

With their vision limited, Everod used his other senses to judge Maura's reactions. He listened to her breathy sighs as the coarse hair on his chest caressed the warm silky curves of her breasts. He touched her face, relieved to discover her cheeks were dry. When he traced her lips with his fingertips, he yelped in surprise when she playfully bit him.

He retaliated by inserting his hand between them, and teasing the nubbin of flesh between her legs as his cock plunged tirelessly in and out of her.

Maura's reaction was instantaneous. She gasped, and her forehead collided with his chin. Grunting, Everod quickened his strokes. Maura squirmed beneath him, her breath rushing between her lips in rapid puffs.

"Give yourself to me," he murmured enticingly into her ear. "It's painless."

Maura thrashed restlessly against him, and then abruptly stiffened. A lady's release was a powerful aphrodisiac. She made a high keening sound, pressing herself against him as he feverishly drove his cock into her over and over.

Sensing his impending release, Everod hastily pulled out of her, his hand closing around the swollen head of his cock. He latched his mouth on one of her nipples, suckling as his hand squeezed and caressed his rigid member. Her breast muffled his gruff shout. Pressing his face into her soft flesh, he stilled as his nimble fingers applied enough pressure to heighten his pleasure. Hot seed pumped from his cock.

"Christ," he exclaimed, when the madness faded from his brain. "I lied about it being painless. Lady, bedding you was the sweetest agony."

He sensed Maura's shy smile.

"Will you be wanting us to do this again?"

Collapsing beside her, Everod groaned. Maura was a siren. His body ached in all the right places, and his damn cock craved more. "Absolutely."

Maybe if they repeated their mad coupling, he could figure out who exactly had surrendered to whom.

CHAPTER 17

"You seem uncomfortable. Do you regret that your aunt could not join us?"

Maura wrinkled her nose at Rowan's question. It was not his company or their lack of chaperone that troubled her. When Rowan had appeared in the breakfast room full of charm and suggested that they explore the park further by horseback, Maura privately winced. Having willingly surrendered her virginity the previous evening, she found the thought of being perched on a side-saddle as a punishment her nether regions could not bear.

Before she could think of a clever reason to refuse his kind offer, Aunt Georgette accepted on Maura's behalf. His invitation also included her aunt, but the countess refused. Worrington's health had not improved, and she wanted to go to Covent Garden to procure some herbs her gardens lacked.

"Not at all. Aunt Georgette's place is at your father's side," she said, happy to focus on matters other than her soreness. "There has been some discussion about summoning a physician; however, my aunt is determined to cure him on her own."

"Well, despite the dreadful flavor of her tinctures,

I must confess I was never ill while residing at Worrington Hall." He shot her a teasing glance. "You will not tell Georgette that I called her concoctions 'dreadful,' will you?"

"Your confession is safe in my care," Maura assured him. "Besides, I do not think anyone in the household considers her medicinal tinctures pleasant."

Rowan laughed, the joyous sound carrying on the breeze. "I am pleased that you accepted my invitation. Earlier, I feared the grounds might be too muddy for a ride this afternoon."

The mention of the storm brought Maura back to the gazebo. Through flashes of lightning, she saw glimpses of their debauched coupling. There was a fierce savagery to Everod's face as he speared his manhood into her frenziedly, until she thought she might die from the pleasure. After a while, Maura no longer heard the rain and the rolling thunder. All she heard was her heart pounding in her ears, the slap of slick flesh, and their hoarse cries of surrender.

Rowan scowled at her expression. "If you are concerned about your mount, my dear, you needn't be. I selected a surefooted gelding for you. No hill or dale will cause it to falter in its task."

"You are very thoughtful, Rowan."

She did not look like a lady who had spent the night in the arms of one of the most notorious of *les sauvages nobles*. Before they had departed for London, her aunt had tossed out Maura's old riding habit, and replaced it with a scarlet redingote, matching half-boots, and a clever black satin hat with a large black plume pinned to the front.

Maura stifled a yawn with her gloved hand.

"A restless night, love?" Rowan asked indulgently. His tone was patronizing enough to make Maura clench her teeth. "Did the storms trouble you?"

"Not as much as I troubled Abbot and the rest of the staff," she said, their horses walking side by side.

Aunt Georgette would not have been able to resist telling Rowan about Maura's nocturnal mischief. Thank goodness, her aunt did not know about Everod or what had transpired in the gazebo as they waited for the rain to diminish.

"I could not sleep, so I took a walk in the gardens. I was caught in the downpour, and tracked mud and water throughout the house," she admitted, still chagrined that her attempts to clean up the mess only smeared her footprints. "Did you not notice Abbot was instructing three maids on the proper method of cleaning the marble in the front hall when we left?"

He signaled his horse to halt when they reached the summit of a hill. She did the same. "Georgette mentioned your penchant for night promenades," he said, leaning forward and giving his horse a friendly pat. "She also mentioned a missing slipper."

Ah, yes, she mused humorlessly. How could she have forgotten her slipper? Clearly, she did not possess the devious mind needed to carry on a clandestine liaison with a lover. Even if she had remembered her slipper, she could not explain away the mud on the floors and her soiled cloak.

Or the loss of my virginity.

Rowan chuckled. "A little like Perrault's *Cendrillon*, don't you think?"

Maura smiled faintly. "Except that my slipper was made of colored kid instead of glass."

Nor did she have a haughty stepmother or stepsisters who were cruel to her. Her serious sea-gray eyes settled on the gentleman beside her. Rowan aspired to be her handsome prince. He was definitely handsome and kind for the appointment. Unfortunately, the man whom she desired craved only her body.

He startled her by grasping her hand. "The next time you walk the gardens at night, I pray you will invite me to join you," he said, his mouth quirking in an endearing manner. "One can never tell what mischief might occur beneath a sky full of stars."

While Rowan courted her niece in Hyde Park, Georgette courted danger in the guise of her handsome stepson Lord Everod. She had come to the decision that a confrontation with her former lover and present enemy was necessary. The man was determined to ruin her schemes.

With luck, age had taught Everod the wisdom of compromise. Perhaps they both could have what they wanted. It was simply a matter of negotiation, and Georgette had worn her favorite dress for such occasions.

It was a pale green muslin dress in which the bodice had been cut lower than just above the bosom, exposing a generous portion of her breasts. When she was concerned about appearances, a white diaphanous scarf was threaded through a slit in the center, and pinned at each shoulder.

Ten years ago, Worrington had given her two

splendid pins that were shaped like leaves. Set with diamonds and emeralds, the pair complemented her dress. When Georgette was feeling informal, she removed the modest scarf from her bosom. Her husband thought she wore her wicked dress only for him. However, there were times when she had sought out other gentlemen.

No man had ever been able to assuage all her desires. At least, not for long.

Everod's manservant Dunley proved no challenge for her. Practically drooling on her cleavage the moment he opened the door, he believed her when she told the servant that Everod had hired her for the afternoon.

It did beg one to ponder exactly what the viscount did with his afternoons.

The servant moved toward the stairs to alert his lordship that his lady friend had arrived. It was all she wanted to know. Georgette stopped the man before he climbed the stairs. Feigning embarrassment, she haltingly explained that Lord Everod had prepared her in advance. Like a Covent Garden actress, she had a part to play and the tale required an element of surprise.

The darling man began stuttering when she accidentally dropped her reticule. Without waiting for the servant to retrieve it, Georgette leaned over and gave him a chance to peek at her breasts. She had no qualms about using her body to gain what she wanted.

When she smiled apologetically at Dunley, the

servant told her precisely which bedchamber belonged to Everod.

Men. They were such adorable simpletons!

When Everod had awakened, the first thing he noticed was the dried blood on his right hand. The tiny smudges were proof that his hours with Maura in the gazebo had not been a dream. There had been other stark reminders of their night together. He discovered another streak of Maura's virginal blood on his inner thigh, several more stains on his shirt that he had used to wipe his spilt seed from his cock.

Everod had promptly dropped the shirt, and summoned Dunley for a bath. He did not feel guilty for claiming Maura's virginity. He might have coaxed her, but the final decision had been hers alone. When they parted, she had kissed him gently on the lips and walked away. If she had not regretted the loss of her innocence, by damn, neither would he.

Freshly clean from his bath, Everod was ready to put Maura from his thoughts for a day. Of late, he had neglected his friends and his clubs. Bedding a lady did not alter his daily routine, and he was determined to stay away from her for a few days. Perhaps if she missed him, Maura would come to him.

Humming to himself, he turned at the soft rustle at the door. Lady Worrington was the last person he expected to see in his bedchamber. "How the devil did you get in here?"

Appreciating that he wore only his breeches, Georgette sauntered into the room. "Rather easily, I must confess. Dunley assumed you hired me for the afternoon."

She circled around him, but he matched her movement, eyeing her as if he had just discovered a viper on the floor. "Honestly, Everod, I must know. Whatever do you do with these women you pay?"

"Play checkers," he snapped, silently cursing his manservant for admitting the only lady he had been tempted to strangle with his bare hands. "Dunley has much to answer for. I pay him well to bar unsavory characters from my residence." He sneered at her. "If you wonder where you rank in my opinion, whores take precedence over you, Lady Worrington."

She sighed, heaving her breasts forward to give him an eyeful. "Tut, my darling man, if you recall, I can be rather perverse. Cruelty in a man only arouses me."

Everod snatched her wrist when she tried to caress his chest. "That's it. You are leaving." Ignoring her struggles, he dragged her toward the door. "I will happily toss your arse into the street."

Georgette sank her teeth into his arm, gaining her freedom. She raced to the door and slammed it shut. Before he could reach her, she had turned the lock and plunged the key down the front of her bodice.

She leaned against the door and gloated.

"Bloody bitch!" Inches above her head, he pounded his fist against the door. "How have you kept my father beguiled for so long? I saw your true nature when I was fifteen."

"Worrington adores me. I fulfill his every whim, and he treats me like a queen!" she said, her blue eyes flashing in triumph.

"While you secretly bed every man who catches your fancy," he said, his voice dripping with disgust.

Her expression softened into something akin to hurt. "I fancied you once, Everod. You were such a beautiful boy. I saw you watching me, too, when your father brought me home. Did you think of me at night when you were alone in your bed? Stroking your cock, your cods tight with anticipation of your release, wishing it was you instead of your father fucking me."

He shook with rage. At least that's what he wanted to believe. The last time Everod had been this close to Georgette, she had teased him into shoving up her skirts while she had unfastened his breeches. Burning with lust, she had parted her thighs and he had betrayed his father without a thought to the consequences. Georgette had a manner about her that drained a man's brain. If Maura and his father had not discovered them together, Everod wondered how deeply Georgette's poison-dipped claws would have scored his flesh.

If one knew where to look, he still bore the faint thin lines where she had marked his back when she had quaked and shivered in his arms. His cock twitched at the potent vision of him pounding himself into her. Horrified that he could be vaguely aroused by her, he stepped away from her.

"What do you want, Georgette?"

Believing she had gained the upper hand, she stalked him. "I propose a truce, Everod."

"Why?"

"Why not?" She shrugged elegantly. "There is no reason to have lies between us. You know that if

Worrington had not learned of our affection for one another, you would still be coming to my bed."

He baldly laughed at her conceit. "You were my first lover, Georgette. There have been others who were prettier, wittier, and definitely cleverer in my bed."

Everod instantly thought of Maura, and the sweet breathy sounds she made when she shuddered in his arms. He would trade one thousand nights with an experienced Georgette and her Machiavellian wiles for one night with Maura. "I barely recall why you appealed to me at all."

"This is about your father, isn't it?" she demanded, believing she understood him. "We were careless. He would never have to learn about our arrangement."

Brazenly moving closer, she pressed her nose against his chest and inhaled. A small sound of pleasure rumbled in her throat. Everod grabbed her by the shoulders and pushed her away, when he felt her tongue lave his flat nipple.

"No, Georgette," he said coldly. "It isn't about my father. This is about you, and what you did to me . . . my family.

"Of course," she said, her expression regretful. "You blame me."

Everod closed his eyes, striving for patience. "I pity you, Georgette. I do not understand how your niece has remained so guileless when she has been nurtured by a manipulative succubus."

"Stay away from Maura!" she shouted, retreating out of his reach.

It was the first genuine reaction Everod had elicited from Georgette. "Why? Are you frightened I might sully the only person who truly loves you? Are you afraid I might convince her to hate you?"

He must have hit on a partial truth. The sleepy-eyed passion she had used to tempt him into resuming their affair had disappeared. Lady Worrington appeared tense and hostile. "I have plans for Maura. Do not interfere. If you cross me, I will use Worrington and anyone else at my disposal to hurt you!"

Georgette squeaked when Everod's hand shot out and caught her just under the jaw. He backed her up until the back of her head struck the door. Her claws were sheathed by kid gloves, so frantic attempts to break his hold were futile. Everod tipped his head to the side as he studied what he viewed as pure evil.

Her beauty was a deadly lure.

Fortunately, he was immune.

"My father should have cut your throat when he pulled me off you, Lady Worrington." He leaned in closer, pleased with the fear he had put in her eyes. "If he is foolish enough to love you, then he deserves his fate. But understand this, approach me again or attempt to malign me or any of my friends, and I will come for you. No one will be able to protect you. When I am finished, you will have a scar to match mine."

Everod tilted his head back so she could see the ugly reminder of what Georgette had cost him. The countess made a choking sound of distress. With his hand still closed around her neck, Everod used his other hand to dispassionately dig into her bodice and extract the key. He held it up in front of her wide eyes. "You may leave."

Georgette snatched the key from his fingers. Giv-

ing him a baleful glare, she jammed the key into the
lock. Seconds later, the door was open. "I hope one of
your damn whores gives you the French pox, you bastard," she said, her bosom heaving with her barely
contained fury. "Keep away from Maura!"

"Too late," Everod mocked too softly for the lady to
hear him. Leaning against the frame of the door, he
watched with indifference as Lady Worrington marched
down the stairs and out of his life.

"Maura is mine to do as I please."

CHAPTER 18

Someone knocked once.

From her prone position on the bed, Maura angled her face toward the door. Who could be bothering her? Aunt Georgette had ordered her to nap for the rest of the afternoon. Her maid should not have bothered her for hours.

The late nights were taking its toll on the family. The earl had been ill for a little more than a week. He continued to complain about a bodily weakness and dull pains in his chest. The weakness had plagued him so much he had not joined them on several of the outings.

Her aunt was concerned. Fearing that the entire household would be overwhelmed by her husband's illness, she had remained in the kitchen for days brewing one of her favorite medicinal remedies, enough to dose the entire household. Aunt Georgette had sent up a tray consisting of tea, buttered toast, and jam to assist in making her bitter herbal tonic palatable.

Maura had nibbled on the toast and dutifully swallowed two spoonfuls of her aunt's tonic, for protesting would not have mattered. In the end, Aunt Georgette always got her way. A single heavy knock rattled the door. She rolled onto her feet to see who was brave enough to ignore her aunt's dictates.

She opened the door.

No one was at the threshold. Puzzled, Maura stuck her head out the door and checked the hall from side to side. The corridor was empty. Was it a prank? Yawning, she stepped back inside and closed the door.

Before she could turn away, she heard the knock again.

Snatching open the door, she hoped to catch the trickster. Maura opened her mouth to scream when she saw Everod in the doorway. The viscount deftly clamped his hand over her mouth and marched her back into the bedchamber.

Maura gaped at him as he closed and locked the door. He had slipped into the Worringtons' town house in the middle of the afternoon. The man's daring bordered on lunacy!

"How did you get into the house unnoticed?" she whispered.

Everod removed his hat, and threw it onto her dressing table. His gloves quickly followed. Lazily, he stalked her as she backed away from him. "It was remarkably easy. I came through the gardens and walked through the door."

"Are you mad? You took an incredible risk," she scolded him. "What if one of the servants had caught you?"

The fire in his amber-green eyes glowed with interest at her state of undress. Since she was supposed to be napping, she wore only her chemise. She thought about the last time he had caught her alone in her nightgown.

Maura trembled.

"I entered with the stealth of a housebreaker, love," Everod said, moving closer when she backed up against one of the posts of her bed.

"If you had been caught, your father would have summoned the constable and demanded that you be charged with trespassing," she said huskily.

Maura did not pull away when he threaded his hand through her long hair. He bent down and inhaled the fragrant strands. "How can it be viewed as trespassing when all of this will be mine one day?"

She could hardly fault his logic. Her pulse quickened when his lips brushed her cheek. "Why did you take such a foolhardy risk?"

"To see you." He grinned at her wide-eyed stare.

Maura pushed at his chest, but the man was too heavy to budge. "I would have seen you at Lord and Lady Kersting's ball."

Everod fingered her puckered nipple through the chemise. "I warrant not like this," he growled, dragging her mouth to his.

His kiss was openmouthed and demanding. Giving up her weak argument, she closed her eyes and leaned against him. When she tentatively touched her tongue against his, he accepted her surrender and deepened the kiss. Everod cupped her left breast in his hand and squeezed. Her tender flesh still bore the faint bruises from their previous lovemaking.

He tore his mouth away, and lowered his head to kiss the exposed flesh of her breast. "Say my name."

"Everod," Maura said softly, her gaze instinctively moving to the door.

The viscount paused, giving her an annoyed look. "My other name. The one I coaxed from your sweet lips as I pleasured you." He grabbed the bottom hem of her chemise and began tugging it upward.

"Townsend," she hastily said, thinking he would cease his teasing and release her chemise.

He pulled the undergarment over her head.

"No!"

Everod gave her a wolfish grin at her protestations. Maura crossed her arms over her breasts. He ran his hand over the length of the chemise, and then twisted it until it resembled a rope. "Who do you think will win this game of wills?"

He seized her wrists, wrapped the fabric around them, and secured them together with a knot. Everod hauled her arms above her head. "Or more importantly, do you really want to deny me?"

Ignoring her protests, he tied her bound wrists to the bedpost. Maura tugged and discovered the knot was tight. She squirmed under his heated stare. "Townsend, untie me. What if someone checks on me?"

"Unless you were anticipating a visit from me—"

"Ha! Your delusions are truly extraordinary."

Chuckling at her aggravation, he traced the outline of her body with his hands. "Your state of undress leaves me to conclude that you were supposed to be resting. I am certain the servants have been ordered not to disturb you," he said knowingly.

"What are you doing?" Maura demanded, her voice

rising as he knelt in front of her. His mouth was inches away from her nether curls.

With his hands on her hips, Everod replied, "Anything I desire."

Maura tested his knots again. He had managed to bind her wrists without hurting her, but she would not be free until Everod decided to release her. She wet her dry lips with a flick of her tongue.

"Enough games," she groaned, when he pressed a kiss to her belly and stood. "If you think to leave me in this embarrassing predicament for my maid to discover me, I—"

His nimble fingers went to his cravat as he glanced at her abandoned tray on the dressing table. "Hush." He undid the knot at his throat, allowing the long ends to dangle down the front of his shirt. "What do we have here?" He picked up the small green glass bottle next to the teapot.

Maura stomped her foot. "Exactly what it seems. Aunt Georgette has been worried about the household succumbing to the illness that ails your father. She is insisting that all of us imbibe her tonic."

"So she still dabbles with her witch brews, eh?" he said, promptly setting the bottle down. "And this?"

"Strawberry jam, you ninny!" Maura curled her fingers around the bedpost and shook it. "If you are hungry, I will send for another tray."

Her stomach fluttered at his wicked smile. He sauntered back to her with the pot of jam. "A tray will be unnecessary when I have a tempting feast in front of me."

Everod placed the pot at the edge of her bed. With his unique amber-green eyes fixed on her face, he pulled the thin leather strip that bound his hair at his nape. Against her will, her nipples constricted into painful nubs as she remembered how his shoulder-length hair tickled the last time he brushed it over her breasts.

Recalling her response, too, Everod cupped her breast. "So sensitive. There is no guile in your responses when I put my hands on you, is there?"

Her body always seemed to react to his proximity. His touch. When he let his hand drop away from her breast, she ached for the loss. "Free me, and I will show you." Maura watched as he removed his coat and laid it on her bed. His shirt was next.

"Later," he said, laughing when she growled at him. He gripped the opposite bedpost to gain some leverage so that he could remove his boots. "You'd make a lovely sacrifice, Maura. A pity I don't worship one of the ancient gods that demanded them."

Everod unbuttoned the falls on his breeches. The waist of his breeches slipped, hanging low on his hips. Through the opening, she had a tantalizing glimpse of the dark whorls of hair. He was aroused, painfully so, she thought, if the large bulge in the front of his breeches was any indication. Everod, however, undressed unhurriedly as if he had all afternoon to tease and play with her.

"So if you have discarded sacrifice for the afternoon, what are your intentions?" Maura asked, her gaze curiously shifting to the small silver pot on her bed.

Grinning, Everod scooped up the pot of strawberry

jam. He dipped his finger into the pot and brought his jam-coated finger to his lips. "Mmm . . . I warrant I can be creative when the mood strikes me."

He plunged his fingers into the jam.

"Everod!" Maura squeaked, when he coated her left nipple with the sticky fruit preserve. "No. No. You go too far!"

"You will be amazed how daring I can be with a willing lady tied to the bed," he countered, a little too politely.

The viscount was not finished painting her body. After he smeared strawberry jam on her right nipple, he dipped two fingers into the silver pot again, and decorated her abdomen with a meandering line down to the nest of curls between her legs.

"Enough," she protested, her terse command ruined with a giggle when he dipped his tongue into her navel to lick away the evidence. "My dress will not require pins or tapes this evening because of your naughty mischief."

Everod stood, uncaring that her jam-covered nipples were marking his chest. "The jam is quite delicious. Taste it." He teased her lower lip until she parted her lips.

Maura closed her eyes, savoring the sweet strawberry jam on her tongue. She moaned as she suckled his sticky fingers. The playful expression on his face sobered at the sensual sound. Withdrawing his fingers from her mouth, he slanted his mouth over hers. A gentle dance with their tongues commenced.

"I usually prefer my jam on toast," she murmured huskily against his mouth.

"Too dry." He pecked her lips, and knelt in front of her. "Too mundane."

Everod nibbled lightly at the curve of her breast, before covering her nipple and areola with his mouth. Maura shivered against the bedpost as he used the flat of his tongue to lave away the strawberry jam from her breasts. "Your flesh definitely improves the flavor of the jam," he mumbled, his hot breath and lips moving down her body. "Certain places of your body are salty, while others are unquestionably spicy."

He dipped his fingers into the pot of jam, and set it on the floor beside them. "I'm a man with a predilection to experiment until I find the right flavor to satisfy my considerable appetites." Everod placed his hand above her knee in a placating gesture. She sensed his goal before he used his thumbs to part her nether lips.

The back of her head collided with the bedpost at the first cool viscous stroke of the jam against the sensitive nubbin tucked within her feminine folds. Impatient to taste her, Everod followed his fingers with his agile tongue, licking away the sweetness.

Her womb clenched as she arched against him, her body vibrating with need. The dampness she had experienced earlier became a hidden hot spring. If her hands had been free, she would have worked her fingers into his hair and pressed his face deeper. "Townsend," she whispered, sighing as his fingers parted her, seeking her womanly sheath.

Everod wiped his wet lips against his upper arm. "Spicy and soothing as sweet honey," he said, slowly rubbing his thumb back and forth in an excruciating manner. "*Amor Veneris, vel dulcedo,* Mateo Columbo dubbed a lady's hidden jewel. Such beauty combined with a lady's soft cries of pleasure tend to inspire a man to honor his discovery with poetical praise."

He lifted Maura's right leg, and placed it on his shoulder. The subtle shift in their positions widened her stance, giving Everod complete control over the pleasure he was wringing from her body.

Oh, the pleasure!

Maura twisted the bindings at her wrists to no avail. Everod understood the workings of her body better than she did. He licked the indentation near her hip and she trembled. He probed and teased the slick satin flesh between her nether lips, driving her to the brink of madness. She was prepared to offer him anything.

"Anything," she sobbed, her breath coming out in gasps.

They both knew what she was asking, nay begging, for.

Only Everod could ease the tension he had deliberately created within her. With her hips moving against his questing mouth and talented fingers, Maura bit her lip to keep from screaming when the first bubble of pleasure exploded. Everod flinched at her muffled shriek. Seizing both hips with his hands, he used his tongue to nuzzle the origin of those delightful ripples, feasting on her excitement like a ravenous beast.

Maura gripped the bedpost for support. Completely vulnerable to him, she closed her eyes and allowed wave after wave of pleasure to buffet her body.

Weakened by his carnal onslaught, Maura stared at him sleepily as she watched him rise like the warrior that Everod was, and hastily shed his breeches.

His thick rod pulsed with its own need to conquer.

Instead of untying her, he turned her so she was facing the bedpost. He positioned her right knee against the soft mattress, while at the same time, he guided his arousal along the crease of her buttocks until he found the heat he sought.

"I've tasted your pleasure," Everod whispered in her ear from behind. "Now I want to feel it squeeze my cock."

His penetration was swift and deep. Maura inhaled sharply, expecting some discomfort, but her body required no coaxing from Everod. His rod moved in and out of her sheath as if he were a part of her.

Maura held on to the bedpost to buffer his frenzied pummeling. Everod had wrapped one arm around her waist, and the other remained buried in her wet nether curls. His teasing demeanor had vanished as he sought his pleasure. Maura could not deny him. Already, the tension he had released earlier was coiling like a spring within her womb. She craved this wild coupling as much as he did.

Everod made a choking sound, and he pressed his face into her shoulder. Maura felt his rod swell within her, before he thrust deeply, holding himself still in her sweet welcoming depths. As he muffled his shout of triumph against her damp skin, she felt the hot jet of his seed fill her.

Shaken by his release, Everod continued tiny, undemanding thrusts while he shuddered against her. Finally, and with reluctance, he withdrew his rod from her sheath. Everod reached over Maura's head, and freed her wrists from the linen bindings.

Maura rubbed her arms and wrists, belatedly becoming aware of the abuse her arms had endured during their lovemaking. Everod picked her up, and tenderly laid her on the bed. Her gaze drifted to his rod, amazed to discover that he was still firm and primed.

Everod climbed on top of her, bracing his arms on each side of her head. "When will your maid wake you?"

"Half past six o'clock," Maura replied, playing with his hair. From this angle, Everod's scar was vulnerable to her perusal, but she kept her face carefully blank. Perhaps he was testing her to see if she would pity him. She sensed that if she acknowledged the scar in any way, Everod would leave her.

Maura did not want him to go. The realization frightened her. She knew better than most that she could not keep him.

Unaware of her thought, Everod kissed her. "Then we have hours yet."

CHAPTER 19

Everod awoke with a start.

For a few precious seconds, he was puzzled by the unfamiliar bed, and then he recalled where he was.

Rolling onto his side, the viscount impassively studied his sleeping lover. Completely relaxed and exhausted by their lovemaking, Maura slept like an innocent child. Even her fist was curled under her chin, a reminder of a long-forgotten habit she had had of sucking her thumb.

She had been full of surprises this afternoon.

Everod had expected Maura to toss him out of her bedchamber when he had arrogantly knocked. Seduction had not exactly been on his mind when he sought her out. He had come to tweak Georgette's nose, though if he were successful, the countess would never learn of his mischief. She had walked into his home uninvited. Everod had merely returned the favor. Georgette had warned him to stay away from Maura.

Everod proved to himself that Maura was his when and wherever he desired her.

Of course, seeing Maura again had caused him to forget about her deceitful aunt. He loved to pique the lady's temper. With luck, he hoped to steal a few kisses from her. When he saw her wearing nothing more than her chemise, Everod could not resist taking her.

She had been charmingly defiant when he had tied her to the bedpost. However, like any passionate lady in her stimulating predicament, she soon was parting her thighs and begging for him to fill her.

Everod had arduously dedicated himself to the gratifying task.

Writhing in desire, Maura was the incarnation of the Greek goddess Hedone, daughter of Eros, the god of erotic love, and the beautiful goddess of the soul, Psyche. In her embrace, for the first time in his life, Everod felt the melding of body and soul. He had even spilled his essence into her, and not cursed his carelessness. Everod softly chuckled. Leave it to Maura to complicate the simple taking of pleasure in a lady's body, he mused. However, Everod could not summon much ire over his predicament.

He was feeling rather tender and indulgent toward the lady who had sated his carnal nature. Everod gently brushed her dark hair from her cheek so he could admire her beauty. Maura opened her eyes, seeming just as confused as he had been upon waking.

She gasped. "Did we sleep too long? What is the time?"

Fearful that they might be discovered, she sat up on her knees.

"Calm yourself," he said, idly caressing her arm. "Your maid won't knock for another hour."

Maura visibly relaxed. "Oh."

"Oh," he mimicked, and crooked his finger, beckoning her closer. "Come here, my little Hedone."

"Your little what?" she said crossly, then recalled her lessons in mythology. "Oh, *her*. I would call you my Eros, but that would make you my father." Maura wrinkled her nose. "Too improper for my sensibilities, though maybe not for you, eh?"

"Maura, love, the last few hours are proof that your sensibilities match mine rather nicely."

Still naked, she crawled over to him, and kissed him. Everod smiled as her hair tickled his face. He guided her left leg over so that she straddled him. "Where can we meet?"

She rolled her eyes at what she viewed as a ridiculous request. "You will see me this evening, Townsend," she said, pleasing him that she used his first name without him demanding it of her. "You are attending Lord and Lady Kersting's ball, are you not? Your father and my aunt will be in attendance, as will your brother, but these events are usually crowded. I am certain we can arrange a walk in the garden or a few minutes alone in the back parlor if you desire."

"Are you content with such a clandestine arrangement?" Everod asked, not understanding the discontentment coursing through him.

"I wager most of your assignations with various ladies of the *ton* were secretive in nature," she teased, bending down to rub her nose against his.

Everod smiled, but the humor of the situation did not reach his eyes. He could not refute that he did not solicit attention when taking a lover. Oftentimes privacy was a necessity in their arrangement, and Everod manipulated the lady's fear of discovery to his benefit. He had treated Maura in a similar fashion, though he was not too proud of his conduct. If he used his former lovers as a guide to the workings of the female brain, Maura should be urging him to make a public declaration by now. To his annoyance, the lady was content to keep their liaison a secret.

As if she planned to sever their intimate connection before he did.

"Who are you trying to protect, Maura?" Everod asked, licking his thumb with his tongue and wiping a smear of jam he had missed near her navel. "You, me, or the family?"

Maura sighed. "Why must I choose just one? I could challenge your motives as well, my lord. Perhaps you seduced me this afternoon with the hope of triggering your father's wrath, or even a challenge from Rowan."

Early on, he had entertained similar fantasies about how he could amuse himself with Maura, and upset his family. However, his motives for visiting her this afternoon were personal, and more convoluted than laying the groundwork for revenge. "I came to you for me, Maura. I desired you, and I claimed you."

Frowning at him, Maura pushed her hair behind her ears. Although she was sitting on top of him and naked, she had the look of a displeased queen conversing with a recalcitrant subordinate. She lifted her right brow at his harsh tone. "My apologies, Lord Everod. How rude of me to question you for sneaking into my bedchamber, tying me to the bedpost, and forcing me to endure the wanton bliss of your mouth, hands, and rod."

Genuine laughter rumbled in his chest. He clutched her hips to prevent her from rolling away. Her haughty recounting of their afternoon together instantly restored his good humor. And ardor. His cock hardened, and ascended until the eager organ bumped her on the buttock, causing her to start.

"Egad, I am beginning to understand how you acquired the intriguing nickname of Ever*hard*!" she gasped, her sea-gray eyes gleaming with barely contained laughter.

Everod gave her buttock a punishing slap. "Disrespectful wench!" he said, rubbing away the sting his hand might have caused. He had no intention of explaining to Maura what he had done with Lady Spryng and Lady Silver to earn the notorious nickname. "Everyone knows there is little truth in rumors."

In spite of Maura's healthy curiosity and passionate nature, he doubted the lady on top of him would understand or approve of the life he had led since he was cast from Worrington Hall.

Maura made a dissenting noise in her throat. "I disagree." She shifted her hips, raising them so his arousal slipped between her legs, deftly finding the portal of her sheath. "Twice you have sated your lust," she said, lowering her lashes while she rocked slowly against him, coaxing him deeper into her body. "And yet, here you are, readying yourself to sheath your rod into me like a sword into a scabbard over and over until I surrender."

"Or I do," he countered as he suddenly thrust to the hilt.

Maura tipped her head back in ecstasy. Her long dark hair flowed down her back, and over his hands, like fine silk. The soft curling ends tickled his taut testicles.

They still had the better part of an hour before Maura's maid would return to awaken her. Everod intended to relish every minute, pushing Maura to the maddening edge of her release, only to deny her until the maid's footsteps could be heard as she approached the door. The risk of getting caught would heighten Maura's pleasure tenfold. When he asked that she meet with him later this evening; she would not refuse him.

Uncle, you look dashing this evening," Maura said, surveying him with a critical eye as she traveled to the Kerstings' town house with her aunt and uncle. "Aunt Georgette's tonic has put color back into your cheeks again."

The earl preened a little under his niece's praise. "Thank you, m'dear. May I return the compliment? There is a sparkle in your eye, and a blush to your cheeks that heralds good health. Knowing my lady well, I assume you and the entire staff were dosed while I recovered in my bed."

Maura was certain the rosy hue darkened at her uncle's casual observation. She credited her high spirits to a lazy afternoon of lovemaking with Everod. His energy and never-ending fascination with her body had left her aching in odd places and ridiculously happy.

"Oh, Maura fussed about taking a nap like she used to when she was a small child," Georgette confided to her husband. "However, I must agree with Worrington. A few hours of rest have vanquished the shadows from under your eyes, my dear, and restored the joie de vivre that has always been a part of your disposition."

"You are too good to us, Aunt," Maura said demurely. She turned away to stare out the window as the coach rolled down the street. Her thoughts often shifted to Everod.

Though she had dozed momentarily in the viscount's arms, Everod was a man of action. There was not a single inch of flesh on her body that he had not claimed with his mouth or hands. Reckless enough to drive her to the brink of insanity, Everod had remained in her bed, making love to her, until the maid's abrupt knock shattered the spell he had woven over them.

Horrified, Maura shouted to the servant that she was awake and required a bath. She tried to crawl away from him, but the viscount had other plans. With the maid on the other side of the locked door, Everod had picked her up effortlessly and slammed her into the soft mattress. Ignoring her struggles, he had wordlessly parted her thighs, plunged his rod into her drenched sheath and rammed himself wildly into her, giving her straightaway the blissful release he had minutes earlier denied her. Fearing the maid might hear her, Maura sank her teeth into his arm as her body writhed under him, burning like a thousand suns. Seconds later, Everod joined her, her sheath milking his rod much as his mouth suckled her swollen breasts.

The viscount had departed as arrogantly as he had entered her bedchamber. Withdrawing his turgid rod from her body, he had retrieved her hopelessly wrinkled chemise and pulled it over her head to cover the evidence of his lovemaking. While she fretted about the maid's return, he had dressed unhurriedly, lingered over their farewell kiss, and then slipped unnoticed from her room.

No one had sounded an alarm, so Everod had apparently escaped the Worrington household unseen. Maura marveled at the viscount's nerve. A small part of her was appalled by her own uninhibited response to Everod. There was something about him that dared her to match his recklessness. In spite of her earlier bath, Maura could smell Everod's essence. Her nether lips were still moist as if her body were preparing for his return.

Maura was expecting Everod to confront her later at the ball, and demand that they meet again in secret. Even now, her womb clenched in anticipation for she did not have the strength to refuse him.

"Maura, did you hear me?" Aunt Georgette asked, her vexed expression hinting that she had tried to engage her niece numerous times before Maura had heard her.

"I beg your pardon, Aunt. You caught me woolgathering," Maura confessed, hoping she seemed contrite.

"A note from Rowan arrived while you were sleeping," her aunt said crisply. "He will be attending Lord

and Lady Kersting's ball this evening, and begs that
you reserve several dances for him."

"Ho!" the earl chortled with glee. "Several dances,
eh? My son is making a public declaration, it appears,
Maura. He is warning the unwedded gentlemen of the
ton of his claim."

Maura smiled faintly at her aunt and uncle. She
thought about the bite mark on her left hip, and the
one hidden on the underside of her right breast.
Everod had made a few claims of his own.

She would have to gather her wits about her if she
hoped to keep the two brothers away from each other.
Both gentlemen seemed to desire her, and that placed
her squarely in the middle of their personal feud.

Their mutual affection for her would not prevent
either man from destroying her if she outwardly
showed her preference for one brother over the other.

Suddenly, the notion of coming down with the earl's
illness seemed preferable to facing either brother.

After Maura had waited her turn in line to greet
Lord and Lady Kersting, it had been Rowan who
had sought her out first. She had been lingering in the
large front hall with Kilby Carlisle, Duchess of Solitea. The poor lady was feeling unwell. A stomach
complaint, the duchess quietly confessed, explaining
that she and her husband were expecting their first
child in late September.

Maura was naturally thrilled for the couple.

Lady Kersting soon joined the two ladies, after
Kilby's sister-in-law, Fayre, had sent their hostess to

aid the young duchess. Having raised ten children of her own, Lady Kersting was sympathetic and promptly invited the duchess to rest in one of the bed-chambers upstairs until her stomach misery waned.

Maura had been about to leave the hall to join the other guests in the ballroom when Rowan touched her on the arm.

"Dare I hope that you were searching for me?" Rowan asked, bowing over her hand.

"I was—" Maura hesitated to reveal the Duchess of Solitea's delicate condition. She did not know if the lady's pregnancy was common knowledge, but she had no intention of gossiping about a lady that she viewed as a friend. "Aunt Georgette had mentioned your note. You asked for a dance, I believe?"

Rowan gestured to the small alcove to the right of the staircase. Between two large pedestals displaying two huge vases stuffed with a colorful array of flowers, a bench for two had been cleverly placed.

"Come let us sit a moment," he invited cordially.

Maura could not think of a reason to refuse him. "Aunt Georgette will be expecting me soon," she warned, giving him a logical reason for them to return to the ballroom.

"Georgette trusts me. Besides, if you have not noticed, your aunt has been earnestly playing match-maker. So arrogant and determined is our Lady Worrington, I fear she has already sent word to your parents that our betrothal is imminent."

"No!" Maura cried out, sinking onto the bench. "Aunt Georgette would not presume to go against my wishes." Her belly curdled at her aunt's betrayal. "No decision has been made. She had no right to write to my parents with this false news!"

Rowan was calm in the face of Maura's ire. He gingerly sat down next to her and took her hand. Maura blinked at their clasped hands. "Maura, no one is conspiring against you. We both have been aware of our family's desire that we marry. For years, I have carefully timed my visits to Worrington Hall when you happened to be visiting. Ours has been a quiet courtship built on years of friendship."

Maura felt cornered and cleverly manipulated by her aunt. She internally seethed at the injustice. While her aunt spoke of time and courtship, Georgette had written her sister and announced Maura's betrothal to Rowan. "Everyone seems so certain of my feelings, Rowan. How could they be when I am not?"

"My father and Georgette were wrong to bring you to London," Rowan said, his somber expression clouded with unspoken concerns he seemed reluctant to share. "Since your arrival, you seem distant and more confused about us. I care for you, Maura. You have feelings for me, too. Do not bother to deny it. Say yes, and I will walk into that ballroom and announce our betrothal."

It was so unlike Rowan to be so determined. Maura blamed her aunt. Most likely, Georgette was behind the young gentleman's earnest declaration.

"I can make you happy, Maura."

She did not want to hurt Rowan, but she was not going to be coerced by anyone. "I asked for your patience, Rowan, and my decision has not changed. I cannot give you my consent."

He seemed to deflate before her eyes. "But your parents," he pressed.

"Will learn when they return to England that Georgette's announcement was premature," she said, knowing her parents had left this marriage business in her aunt and uncle's hands because they could not be bothered. "Either way, they will support my decision."

Rowan nodded, understanding that if he continued to pressure her, she would flatly refuse him. "You have not discouraged me. Pardon my frankness, but I am determined to have you, Maura. I will not give up. If I must follow you back to Worrington Hall, I will."

Maura suspected as much. She remained seated when he stood. "I can be terribly stubborn, Rowan. Give me the time I need to make my own decision."

They were at an impasse. Rowan tactfully retreated.

"Dance with me later?" he asked, attempting to lighten the tension between them.

"Of course."

Rowan took several steps, and then pivoted toward her. "Oh, I almost forgot. When I was searching for you, Georgette summoned me to her side and inquired as to your whereabouts. She would like you to join her in the ballroom."

"I will. Thank you, Rowan."

Maura watched as Rowan walked away. She itched to confront her aunt immediately, but their conversation would have to wait until after the ball.

"It's a good thing Rowan refrained from kissing

you after his touching speech," Everod mused aloud from somewhere over her head. The arrogant rogue must have been on the stairs shamelessly listening to her and Rowan's private conversation. "Regardless, I'm still tempted to seek him out and bloody the sniveling puppy's nose."

CHAPTER 20

Maura jumped to her feet and whirled around, backing up to find Everod. She found him leaning negligently against the railing on the stairs. His stance might have been casual, but there was a hint of something menacing in his gaze.

Eyes of a hunter, came the unbidden thought.

"Gentlemen who have the nasty habit of eavesdropping on private conversations tend to hear admissions that are unpalatable," she said, her hands clenched at her sides. "Were you spying on me, Lord Everod? Think carefully before you reply."

Maura was in no mood for the viscount's games. Although he could be playful as he had been earlier in her bedchamber, she would not fool herself into believing that Everod could not be ten times as ruthless as her aunt. She was surrounded by people who wielded words and people as skillfully and effortlessly as a foil, and Maura had the good sense to know she could be trumped by all of them.

His left palm glided down the smooth polished surface of the railing as he descended the staircase to join her in the alcove. "I was merely enjoying Lord Kersting's hospitality, when I accidentally overheard my brother's tepid declaration of affection and desire to pledge himself to you." Everod grimaced as if recalling the painfully awkward exchange between the couple. "Your ambiguous reply was equally humorous. Why are you hesitating, Maura? Holding out for a better offer?"

Outraged that the viscount could mock her confusion and desire not to hurt Rowan so thoughtlessly, Maura gave him a hard shove. Everod took a step backward only to placate her.

"You inconsiderate, pompous cretin!" she said, keeping her voice at a pitch that did not carry beyond the alcove. "At least your brother's intentions are honorable. I do not see you on your knees, Townsend, offering your heart along with your colossally remarkable virile member!"

She would be lying to herself if she did not privately admit that it stung her pride, knowing that Everod viewed her no differently than the legions of lovers he had seduced over the years. Like the ladies before her, Maura had secretly longed to tame his feral heart, but it was for naught. Everod would never permit himself to be vulnerable to another person, least of all trust the fickleness of a lady's affection.

Everod startled her by seizing her by her upper arms and shoving her up against the wall. One of the nearby vases wobbled slightly at the impact. His lips hovered temptingly near hers. "I do not recall you complaining about my virile cock as I vigorously plunged into your sweet, enchanting quim. In fact, you begged me to thoroughly fu—"

Maura silenced him with an impulsive kiss. She

would not allow him to liken their lovemaking to rutting beasts satisfying a mutual instinctive need. Everod had touched more than her body, though he would probably laugh at her lack of sophistication.

Everod had initially stiffened when she rose up on her toes and stemmed his insulting depiction of their afternoon together. His indifference was blessedly brief. Pressing the length of his body aggressively into her, Everod took control of the kiss she had initiated. His tongue possessively slipped into her mouth, forcing her to accept his physical claim. Maura did not shy away from his dominance. She brazenly tangled her tongue with his, reminding him that his control was tenuous.

Drawing back, Everod lowered his forehead against hers. "Maura, love, you know how to spoil a perfectly good fight," he chided, though he did not seem particularly upset. "All I want to do is steal you away into the night and remind you of how wicked you can be when you are not trying so hard to be good."

"And I might have let you, if Aunt Georgette were not expecting me to join her in the ballroom," Maura said, laying her gloved hand against his cheek. She exhaled, gazing at him wistfully. "Oh, Townsend. Why do you persist in testing my loyalties, and then become angry when I refuse to hurt those I view as family."

Everod kissed the small patch of skin between her eyebrows. "Perhaps I dislike the people who lay claim to your loyalty and affection. They are unworthy, and you seem deliberately blinded to their faults. Are you seriously considering the puppy's offer of marriage?"

"What lady would not contemplate a genuine offer

of marriage?" she countered, feigning surprise at his obtuseness. "Nevertheless, I believe I lack the proper temperament to be a good wife to your brother."

If only she could convince Rowan of that without hurting his feelings.

"A wise decision," Everod said, kissing her again. "May I be present when you reject him?"

Maura rolled her eyes heavenward. She slipped under his arm, moving away from him. "I wish you were jesting. Rowan does not deserve your condescension or hatred."

Everod caught her by the wrist. "He would earn both if he managed to coax you into marriage," he said, pulling her closer. He picked her up and carried her deeper into the alcove.

"Put me down!" she said, laughing. "Someone might see us together."

"Not if we are quiet," he murmured, tipping her chin upward to gain access to her pouting lips.

Neither Everod nor Maura noticed Rowan standing ten yards away from them. Though the large bouquet of flowers hid his presence from the amorous couple, Rowan was certain he could knock the vase off the pedestal and still not betray his position.

His hands clenched into impotent fists as he glimpsed his brother's hand curl possessively around Maura's hip. Damn them both, he thought, seething in mute fury. From their intimate embrace, Rowan deduced Everod had bedded Maura. He had stolen his future bride's virginity, and likely her heart, for Maura would not have succumbed to the scoundrel's charms unless the man had rekindled her affection.

Her innocence was mine to claim!

Georgette would be as livid as he was over this latest development. She was insistent that Rowan marry her niece. He had been agreeable, even looked forward to marriage. His brother, once again, had ruined everything. When had Everod seduced Maura? How long had the couple been mocking him while he had been unaware of their betrayal?

Rowan ground his teeth at Maura's soft laughter. While she seemed so reluctant to acknowledge her tender feelings for him, Maura had willingly surrendered her virtue to one of London's most notorious rakes.

He had seen enough.

Retreating as silently as he had approached the alcove, Rowan knew what had to be done as he headed back to the ballroom. It was apparent Maura was too innocent to understand that Everod was merely using her. Over the years, people had whispered into his ear, regaling him with tales of the viscount's carnal conquests, his numerous duels, and perchance of mischief with the other members of *les sauvages nobles*.

Georgette had often expressed her desire that he marry her niece to protect her from Everod. Rowan now understood the countess's concerns. Maura needed him. She would not initially appreciate his high-handedness, but with time, her gentle nature would overcome her anger. She would eventually forgive him.

If he had taken a bolder path, he might have spared her his elder brother's lust.

Rowan would seek Georgette's sage counsel before he took action.

It was time for Everod to understand that he could not lay claim to all that he coveted.

Dallying with Maura in the alcove had restored Everod to his former good humor. He had behaved himself to the best of his abilities. He had satisfied himself with a few lingering kisses, and a playful squeeze on her lovely backside before he had turned her loose.

Georgette had summoned her niece, and Maura was too devoted to openly defy the countess. He trailed after Maura, content to observe her from a distance.

Before she had run off, Everod had gained her breathy consent that they would meet later in Worrington's gardens. He was of the mind to kidnap her, taking her back to his town house where her cries of pleasure could be uninhibited while his frenzied thrusts repeatedly drove her to her womanly climax.

Sensing his presence, Maura halted and gazed back at him.

"Go away." She mouthed the words, somewhat exasperated with him because she sensed that he would not heed her command.

Maura was astute.

She slipped into the crowd, weaving her way to join his family.

The lady could not dismiss him so easily, especially since he was not finished with her. As he worked his way through the crowd, there was a rousing cheer in the direction Maura had been heading.

Over the fanciful sea of feathers, jewels, and silk,

Everod watched as two gentlemen hoisted Rowan high onto their shoulders. His brother had a bottle of wine in one hand, and a glass in the other. Shouting out for everyone's attention, Rowan clanked the glass against the bottle.

"I beg for your patience," Rowan shouted over the murmurs of curiosity. "And your ear." His handsome features beamed with elation as he noticed Maura off to the right of the small group of people his antics had drawn. "There you are, my dear. Come, join me." He extended his hand.

Everod moved forward, but his gait slowed as he noted Maura's puzzlement, and increasing unease from being the center of attention. He was so focused on Maura that he did not immediately notice the two gentlemen who deliberately blocked his way.

It was Solitea and Cadd.

Both gents looked grim, which did not bode well for him.

"Don't." The duke's soft entreaty made the fine hairs at the back of the viscount's nape bristle.

His friends knew something. What had they overheard before Maura had been summoned? "Out of my way," Everod growled, attempting to brush by them. If they wanted to fight him in front of a room filled with guests, he would oblige them. He was not particularly concerned about the ensuing scandal.

"This business is done," Cadd said tightly, as he grabbed Everod by the arm. He might have cuffed the marquess for his impudence if Rowan's words had not shifted the ground from beneath his feet.

"I have news to share, and I cannot wait for the papers!" his brother said, staring at Maura. "Raise your glasses, my friends, and drink heartily for I have joyous tidings. With the blessings of both our families, four weeks hence Miss Keighly will become my bride!"

The bride in question furiously blushed at Rowan's announcement. She tried to speak, but her voice was drowned out. Amid the cheers and toasts, dozens of well-wishers pressed forward to congratulate the couple.

Everod shoved Cadd's restraining hands away, his scorching hot gaze focused on Maura's deceitful beautiful face. Hours earlier, she had lain in her bed, sleepy and replete from their lovemaking. As she had parted her thighs, writhing and pleading for him to fill her, she had whispered that she was his alone. Moments earlier in the alcove, she had sworn that Rowan would not gain her consent.

She had lied.

The similarities between Maura and her aunt were not lost on Everod. As if sensing his approach, Lady Worrington saw his savage expression and smiled.

The countess was savoring her victory.

An unyielding grip hauled him backward. Everod turned and snarled at Solitea's interference. "Hands off!"

"You've had your revenge," the duke said, his voice low with tension. "Let her go. She deserves to make a life for herself, to marry a decent gentleman who will give her a dozen kids, and try to make her happy. If you have any tender feelings for the young lady, you will stay away from her."

Tender feelings? What he felt for Maura was dark

and volatile, twisting and fuming just beneath the surface. The thought of her made him yearn. His chest was so tight he thought his lungs might implode; his brain buzzed with reckless feverish thoughts. Solitea thought he had had his revenge on Maura and his family. His friend was wrong. Maura's betrayal had tipped the scales once again, and Everod was determined to return the favor.

"We'll leave after I've made my toast to the future bride and groom," he said, his lips contorted in a frightening distortion of a smile. With a fluid grace he slipped Solitea's hold, and he moved away, ignoring his friend's muttered oaths.

Seizing a bottle of wine from one of the male revelers, Everod raised the bottle as he faced Rowan and Maura. "I would also like to offer a toast."

Lord Worrington subtly shifted so he was standing between his two sons. The protective gesture was further proof his father viewed him as the villain. "This is a happy event, Everod. Your drunken rambles are not wanted here."

Everod shifted his jealous, brooding gaze from his father to Maura. Her eyes brilliant with unshed tears, she was the only one who looked him directly in the eye. Chin tilted upward, she was struggling to hold her composure. There was a despairing resignation in her expression, as if she knew what he was about to do, and was helpless to stop him.

"Let him speak his toast," Rowan, the favored son, said and Everod's fingers itched to punch his brother for his charity. "You have tender words for me, Brother?"

The benevolent victor surrounded by family and friends did not fear anyone, least of all his outcast brother. Everod took a breath and savored the moment. Rowan had sorely underestimated his opponent.

"You don't have to do this," Cadd hissed in the viscount's ear.

Everod disagreed.

Neither Cadd nor Solitea understood. They thought he was striking out in jealousy. His feelings were a trifle more complicated than that. His friends did not fully comprehend what Georgette's carnal machinations had cost him. He did not give two farthings for his virginity. If he had been left to his own designs, he would have tossed his innocence away on a milkmaid or a pretty whore selling her fleshy wares in some tavern.

Georgette had seduced him, partly out of desire and power. However, her true aim had been so vile and ruthless, even he would have never guessed the lady's hidden nature. He had had years to ponder the malicious actions of his stepmother.

In hindsight, the answer was evident. Georgette had viewed him as a threat. Everod had been curious about his father's new wife in those early months, and he had discreetly watched her. Once he had caught her kissing one of the grooms. Twelve years ago, Everod's opinion held sway with his father, and time would have only strengthened that bond. Fearing that he might recount the incident to his father, Georgette turned her ample wiles on him. She had appealed to his pride and lust, and Everod had sweetly succumbed to her lures, allowing the countess to entice him into committing a betrayal his father would never forgive, one that almost ended Everod's life.

And Maura?

Please.

She did not mouth the word as she had before when she playfully attempted to dissuade him from following her. He saw the plea in her liquid gaze. Everod deliberately looked away, dismissing her.

For some reason, not entirely clear to him, Georgette wanted Maura to marry his younger brother. It was important to Lady Worrington that the marriage transpire. So important, Everod was equally determined to snatch the prize from her. His brother would not marry Maura Keighly.

His revenge would cost a lady her honor.

"Aye, I do, Rowan Lidsaw," Everod said, his voice silencing the chatter around him. "I congratulate you, Brother. Your lady is exquisite."

Everod gestured at Maura without meeting her eye. "Beautiful . . . educated . . . strong bloodlines . . . and skin so soft, it inspires a man to stroke it and spout ridiculous verses." He raised the bottle higher, as he grinned at Georgette. "I am *intimately* acquainted with her exceptional qualities," he purred smoothly, switching his attention to Rowan. "She surrendered her innocence to me with a generosity and enthusiasm you will come to appreciate when you fu—"

Rowan slammed his fist into Everod's jaw.

The viscount staggered back, colliding into several witnesses to the Worringtons' latest debacle. Someone steadied his stance. Distantly Everod heard several ladies scream and the ballroom seemed to erupt in utter chaos. His father grabbed Rowan from behind and was struggling to hold him. Clutching the front of her bodice as if frightened, Georgette watched them all, her excitement barely contained.

Maura had vanished like a specter.

Everod rubbed the sting out of his jaw as he searched for her. He tasted blood, too, but he would never admit the blow had hurt. "You hit like a spoiled puppy, Little Brother. On second thought, maybe you are not man enough to bed a lady like Maura—"

Rowan roared, tore himself free from Worrington's grasp, and launched himself at his brother. Everod relished the fight. The fact that Rowan had planned to marry Maura was reason enough to bloody the man's pretty face. Everod wanted to gouge, pummel, and rend until there was nothing left.

It took Solitea, Ramscar, and Cadd to pull him away from his brother. Two gentlemen were helping Worrington hold Rowan down. His brother was raging, flailing about, as he demanded that his captors free him.

"Enough!" Solitea shouted at Everod. "This is finished. You've done what you came for."

Solitea had taken part in countless brawls and duels. The man's condescending tone was damn irritating, and Everod was in no mood for hypocrites. "And what was it I came here for, *Your Grace?*"

Something wild flashed in Solitea's green eyes. A muscle near his mouth jumped. Everod tensed, expecting his friend to strike him down. "Revenge on your family, though if you want my opinion, I think you punished the wrong person."

"What do you know?" the viscount said sullenly. Maura had become his lover, but she had been quietly planning to marry his younger brother.

"I know that you announced to half the *ton* that Maura Keighly, Lord and Lady Courtwill's *daughter,* was your eager whore. Honestly, Everod, cutting the lady's throat would have been merciful."

"*Biche-sone,*" Everod murmured under his breath, uncertain if he was referring to himself or Solitea. Swinging his hands out to push away his well-meaning friends, he staggered away from his family who were still cursing his name.

M aura could not remember how she managed to cross the large ballroom. One moment she was staring at Everod, mutely appealing to him not to confirm her secret fears that she had meant nothing more to him than a way to hurt his family, and the next she was striding through the door that opened into the front hall.

With her hand at her throat, she dragged air into her lungs praying she would not add to her humiliation by fainting. People stared and whispered as they passed her, but no one paused to ask if she was ill.

Oh, how her heart ached!

The pain was simply intolerable. Blinded by her unshed tears, she covered her mouth with her hand and sobbed.

"Maura!"

She heard someone speak her name several times before she reacted. By then, she felt someone hug her. Maura blinked several times to clear her vision.

It was Kilby.

"Maura, what happened?" the duchess asked gently.

Had she not witnessed Everod's revenge? The viscount had been ruthless and quite thorough in his attack. Kilby had missed a performance worthy of the stage. Hysteria bubbled up, clogging her throat with misplaced laughter.

"Everod," Fayre spat, her shoulders quaking with her ire. "If Fayne does not murder the scoundrel for what he has done, I surely will."

"And I will help you!" Kilby said, hugging Maura too tightly. "Maura, you are coming home with us." She did not give Maura a chance to argue. To Fayre, she said, "We can leave word with one of the servants so the Worringtons know her whereabouts."

"The men can find their own way home. I think it prudent that we depart immediately," Fayre said, nodding at the ballroom doors.

The notion of confronting Everod again allowed Maura to shake off the numbing stupor that was claiming her. With her friends flanking her, and issuing terse orders to the hovering footmen, they hurried out of the house.

CHAPTER 21

"Madam, leave my coat alone," Worringon bellowed at his wife. "If I wanted my damn valet, I would have summoned him."

Espying his mistress, her Blenheim spaniel Beau ambled with his head low toward her, his nails clicking on the hardwood flooring. Unfortunately, the poor creature made the mistake of crossing in front of Worrington. Almost stumbling, the earl swore and kicked the animal on his rump. Beau yelped and scurried under the bed.

"Devil take the beast! I grow weary of tripping over it," he said, removing his coat out of sheer obstinacy, and throwing it at her dog.

Oh, her husband was in a fine fury. It was amazing the walls of the coach had not toppled as the earl pounded his fists against them, thundering curses at his elder son, and anyone else who had the misfortune to encounter him.

"Beau wanted some affection from you, my lord," Georgette said, wishing she had the luxury of kicking anything or anyone she desired. The evening had seemed so promising, after Rowan had agreed to announce his betrothal to Maura. She had anticipated

Maura being skittish about a betrothal to which she had not officially agreed. However, her niece would have resigned herself to her fate. Everod would have eventually discarded her as a lover. Even if Maura had fancied herself in love with the scoundrel, she would have come to accept that not many gentlemen would have overlooked her lack of virtue.

What Georgette had not anticipated was Everod's public attack on Maura. The man had been savagely cruel. If it had not been *her* plans he was ruining, Georgette might have applauded his efforts. She had sorely underestimated Everod. She had assumed his seduction of her niece would have satisfied his need for revenge. Why would the man care who his brother married? It should have amused Everod that Rowan was marrying a lady the viscount had privately taught the bed skills of a practiced courtesan.

Georgette did not understand Everod's reasoning. That in itself made him a very dangerous man. This evening it became clear that Everod would not be satisfied until his hands were stained with her blood.

"My love," she said, coming up to her husband and placing both hands on his face. "Your coloring concerns me. I should not have encouraged you to leave your bed. You are not well."

She was not exaggerating. His face looked chalky, even his lips. There was a fine tremor to his body that she had initially mistaken for rage. He was also perspiring, though the room seemed cool to her.

Some of the anger waned as Worrington gently pulled her hands away from his cheeks and brought them to his heart. "I feel weak, Wife," he grudgingly admitted. "I loathed to tell you, when my family needs me."

Georgette brought their joined hands to her lips and kissed his knuckles. Maura had run off before anyone thought to stop her. After Everod had swaggered away, Worrington and his male companions had released Rowan. Shouting curses at all of them, he had disappeared into the crowd. It was too much to hope that Rowan might have the courage and skill to hunt down his elder brother and slay him for his troublemaking.

Worrington swayed, brushing against her. "I need to find Rowan."

"What you need is one of my tonics and strong tea," Georgette replied sternly, tugging on his hand until he followed her to the bed. He wearily collapsed on the bed. "I will ring for your manservant to undress you. Rowan will return when his temper has cooled. You bruised his pride by treating him like a little boy who needed protection from his older brother."

"I had to do something," he muttered, sliding onto his back. "You saw them. Both obstinate and furious, each was preparing to murder the other. My sons . . ." Worrington closed his eyes.

Georgette pursed her lips in contemplation. *My sons.* This was the first time in years that she had heard him acknowledge that he had two sons. Although he would deny it, Worrington was worried about Everod, too. "I will bring your medicine, love,"

Georgette said, kissing him on the lips. "Soon the pain and weariness will melt away."

I thought he loved me."
    Curled up on the Duke and Duchess of Solitea's sofa in the drawing room with a thick woolen throw tucked in around her, Maura wondered if she would ever feel warm again.

"Oh, he could not bring himself to say the words. Too much pride, I told myself. Too many lies spoken for either of us to trust wholly," she said, trying to explain to the three solemn ladies who sat beside her why she had yielded to a gentleman who had carelessly humiliated her with no thought to what he had done to her.

Patience leaned over and poured more tea into her cup. She had arrived at the house twenty minutes after them. Though she had been in the ballroom with her husband, the couple had been dancing when Rowan had surprised everyone, including Maura, with his marriage proclamation. When fighting broke out between the two brothers, Ramscar had literally dragged her away from the chaos and ordered her to wait in the card room. Maura, Kilby, and Fayre had already departed by the time Patience had reached the front hall.

"If I had known what Everod's plans were, I would have given him a helpful shove toward Mr. Lidaw's raised fist!" Patience said, displaying a rather fascinating bloodthirsty nature. "It must have been so awful, standing there while he praised your—your—"

"My assets," Maura said, finishing what Patience

was too kindhearted to say. "High praise, I suppose, from a man who has bedded a staggering number of ladies."

Fayre frowned. "Everod never struck me as a cruel man. What he did this evening was reprehensible." She muttered something unintelligible and dug her handkerchief from her reticule. "I do not understand any of this. I saw how Everod behaved around you. I could have sworn the man had finally fallen in love."

A love he willingly sacrificed for revenge.

Maura set her cup of tea aside. Once Kilby and Fayre had hustled her into the Solitea coach, she had succumbed to the tears she had fought back in the ballroom. With the comfort of friends, her grief finally breached the emotional dam that had been held together by sheer will alone. In the dark interior, Maura had grieved for the man she had loved. After an hour, she had nothing left. Her insides felt sickly and hollowed.

"Oo-oh, I am so disappointed in Everod!" Kilby said, so distressed by what had occurred, she could sit only for a few minutes at a time. "The man should be gelded!"

"Forthwith, I am ordering Hedge to put all the knives under lock and key," the Duke of Solitea said, entering the drawing room.

All four ladies turned toward the door.

The duke was not alone. Maura's stomach clenched at the realization that Everod could have joined his friends. Mr. Brawley, Lord Byrchmore, and Lord Ramscar crossed the threshold greeting the ladies. She stared at the empty doorway for a few seconds, silently telling herself that she was relieved that Everod had not sauntered into the room with a cocky grin on his face and an apology that she would toss in his face.

Kilby glared at her husband. When the duke attempted to kiss her on the cheek, she tilted her face away. "If I told our butler the bitter tale of what transpired this evening in the Kerstings' ballroom, the man would take up a knife to help me geld your friend."

His Grace straightened with a sigh hissing from his lips. He cast a guarded glance in Maura's direction. "You heard about Everod's mischief. I suspected as much when I learned you had departed the ball without telling me. I was worried that our babe had made you ill."

"I am ill. However, you can thank Everod for my upset," Kilby said, poking him in the chest.

"Christ, you have bony fingers!" The duke took several steps back. "I can tell you are upset, but you are attacking the wrong man."

"All of you are his friends," Fayre said, dabbing at her eyes. "I cannot believe none of you thought to stop him."

Hesitant of her reaction, Mr. Brawley slowly sat down beside his wife and took her hand. "You should have no quarrel with me, Wife. I wasn't in the ballroom."

"And I was dancing with Patience when Everod decided to make an arse out of himself," Ramscar said, sounding disgusted by the viscount's actions. "Once I stashed Patience somewhere safe, I rushed to where the fight was occurring. Hell, I did not even know Everod was in the thick of things until I saw Cadd and Solitea drag him off Rowan Lidsaw."

The gentlemen were keenly aware that the lady who had been subject to their friend's cruelty was sitting quietly on the sofa. No one seemed to be able to look Maura in the eye, as if they blamed themselves for the viscount's actions.

"You must have sensed something was amiss," Patience said, allowing her husband to put his arm around her and cuddle her against his side. "Ram, you mentioned that Solitea and Cadd were close enough to drag Everod off his younger brother." The blonde appealed to Lord Byrchmore, who was closest to her. "Did something upset Everod?"

It was Solitea who replied. "He was a mite perturbed when Lidsaw announced that he was marrying Miss Keighly."

"I saw his face," Lord Byrchmore added, rubbing his neck. It was obvious Maura's presence was making him feel uncomfortable. "He looked like a man who had taken a blow to the breadbasket. He seemed—" The marquess nodded at Maura, silently inquiring to the others the wisdom of their discussion.

"Pray continue, Lord Byrchmore." Maura spoke for the first time, her voice husky from crying and disuse. "How did Lord Everod seem to you?"

She had not seen Everod's face when Rowan had announced their betrothal. However, the man could not have been more stunned by the announcement than Maura had been. Rowan had grown dissatisfied with her hedging when he spoke of marriage. She had thought that she could delay, put him off until the season's end. His boldness still astounded her.

Lord Byrchmore stared down at his shoes. "Savage, Miss Keighly. We tried to get him to leave." He mutely beseeched Solitea for support. "Everod would not listen to us."

Kilby gasped, shifting her horrified gaze from the marquess to her husband. "You guessed his intent and did not stop him?"

"We tried! Everod refused to heed our warnings," Solitea shouted defensively at his wife. "This is family business, Kilby. One must tread with care when interfering."

"Out!"

"I beg your pardon," the duke asked, his voice quieting as his own temper flared.

Kilby pointed at the door. "You heard me, Fayne. Leave us. Your sympathies apparently lie with your friend, and I happen to disagree, which makes *you* not my favorite person this evening. Lord Everod is a vile miscreant."

"Hell, Little Wolf," he yelled, using an endearment he had given her that had been derived from her former surname, Fitchwolf. "I agree with you! I would have beaten the man bloody if he hadn't stormed out of the Kerstings' ballroom."

Maura stirred in her seat. She did not want Kilby to toss her husband out of his own house because of her. Everyone else seemed to be transfixed on the arguing couple.

"Please, Kilby," she entreated the duchess. "There is no need to throw a man out of his own house because you do not agree with him. Think of your child. This upset cannot be good for the baby. Besides, I have tarried here too long. I should return to my aunt and uncle, and face—"

"No!" the three ladies protested in unison.

The Duke of Solitea stared at Maura, his keen green eyes noting her tearstained face and the utter misery his friend's outburst had triggered. And yet, she thought of his wife's health and that of their child. He nodded, a belated respect kindling in his expression. "No, stay. We'll go."

The duke addressed his wife. "This is the first of many calls this eve. I insisted that we stop here first because you had left the ball without word to me. I was worried," he said gruffly, clearly not pleased that his friends were witnessing how gentle he could be with his duchess. He lightly splayed his hand on her stomach to remind her that both she and the child growing in her womb were important to him.

"Where are you going?" Kilby asked, leaning against her husband as if their brief fight had weakened her.

"After Everod," His Grace replied, needing her to understand. "He is out there somewhere, and we need to find him before he decides to take his anger out on any unfortunate bastard who crosses his path."

Fayre touched her hand to her throat in a protective gesture. "Is he that dangerous?"

Mr. Brawley patted her hand and stood. "He has no quarrel with us."

Ramscar kissed Patience on the lips. "If he encounters Lidsaw again, the pair may finish what was started in the ballroom," Ramscar grimly interjected. "Wait for me here."

Maura pulled the blanket tucked around her higher, and averted her face as the gentlemen bid their farewells to their wives. She noted that Lord Byrchmore, the only bachelor in the room, also seemed disconcerted by what should have been private between the couples.

Her thoughts returned to Everod. Although the viscount had devastated her this evening, she could not quell the growing concern welling within her. Even his friends were worried about what he might do. Everod was prowling the streets of London, angry and reckless. If his friends did not find him, he might be injured, mayhap killed.

Maura could not bear the thought.

Not when it would deprive her of the pleasure of killing him herself.

CHAPTER 22

"This is most unexpected."

Everod glanced up from his pot of beer to study the lady standing in front of him. Uninterested in cards, Everod had selected a table in one of the dark corners of the gaming hell. He had wanted to be alone, but he was reconsidering his decision.

"So are you, my bonny girl." He kicked out a chair so that she could sit with him. "Shall I summon a barmaid for another pot or do you prefer something else?"

She giggled, cocking her head so the ribbons and tiny bells threaded in her brown-colored tresses jingled. Since she was a barmaid, she couldn't very well carry out the task for which she had been employed, and simultaneously flirt with the gentleman she hoped would increase her earnings for the evening.

"What if we just share," she said with a merry smile as she gingerly picked up his pot and sipped the beer. She stared at him over the rim. "You seem lonely."

Everod was startled by the lady's astuteness. He had been musing about his life, and how alone he felt, even though the hell was crammed to the rafters with professional gamblers, loutish young noblemen who preferred the stews to elegant drawing rooms, sailors, drunks, and whores. Giving her a practiced smile, he shrugged. "No more than any other man, I suppose."

"Oh, I know for a fact that you do possess more than the average man, my lord," she cooed, offering him the pot. "I remember you. More to the point, are you willing to share it with me again?"

Everod peered at the young woman's face. He did not recognize her. She had a sweet face, with rosy cheeks and sparkling dark blue eyes, but she was not beautiful. He did not look at her and hunger.

She wasn't Maura.

"We have met, then?" he said, lifting his brow questioningly. Had he been so shallow in his couplings with other ladies that he had not bothered to learn their names or recall their faces?

Or had Maura banished his earlier conquests, wiped them from his mind so that he would only think of her? Everod could almost convince himself that Maura Keighly was an enchantress. He had been beguiled by her the moment he approached her at the bookseller's shop.

The barmaid's pout was emphasized by the red rouge painted on her lips. "Oh, love, you don't recall loving poor Marjorie? We had a grand time, you and me in the back. You rented one of the private rooms. Told Xavier you were showing me some trickery with cards. A leg-ger-man—" She scowled as she tried to recall the word he had used.

"Legerdemain," he smoothly corrected, amused that he had seduced the wench with a word she had not understood let alone could pronounce. "And did my nimble tricks please you, Marjorie?"

The barmaid nodded enthusiastically. "Aye, my lord." Pressing her advantage, she slid from the chair and moved to his lap. "You were most generous. After I finish my duties, I wouldn't mind another one of your lessons in the back rooms."

Everod flicked one of the little bells in her hair, and smiled absently at the faint jingle. He must have been quite foxed to have risked Xavier's wrath by using the hell as his personal brothel. Though he could not recall Marjorie, she would have appealed to his lusty nature. She had a fair face, was plump in all the right places, and her eagerness for his coin would have made up for what she lacked.

The barmaid brazenly nestled her hand between their bodies and rubbed the bulge at the apex of his breeches. Everod was not surprised his cock warmed and thickened at her brisk strokes. "Oh, my, you are a big man," she said, her eyes shining with approval.

She leaned closer and kissed him. Everod did not pull her away, but he did not encourage the barmaid by kissing her back. She tasted of the beer she sold, and there was a slight bitter aftertaste from the rouge she had painted on her lips. Marjorie took his hand, and brought it up to her breasts.

"I seem to recall you were partial to these, my lord," she purred in his ear.

With Marjorie wiggling in his lap, Everod could not deny that his nether regions were responding as God intended. He was not made of stone, though his straining cock was determined to make a liar out of him. Later, when he reflected on this moment, he would laugh. He had a willing, amorous female in his

arms, and Everod felt nothing. No curiosity. No excitement. No desire to take the comely barmaid into a
private room in an attempt to erase Maura's touch
from his brain.

It was a sad predicament.

Y our Grace," Hedge said from the threshold. "A
gentleman is in the front hall. He begs for an audience."

Everod.

Maura straightened in her seat, glancing about for
a way to escape the confrontation.

Kilby frowned at the servant. "At this hour? Who
is it?"

"A Mr. Lidsaw. His unpleasant connection to Lord
Everod urged me to shut the door in the man's face.
However, he claims to be betrothed to Miss Keighly."
The butler sniffed, a not-so-subtle pronouncement of
his personal opinion. "Shall I throw him out?"

The servant's loyalty was to the Soliteas, and that
included Everod since he was a treasured friend.
Maura glanced at Kilby, but she had come to a decision on her own.

"Send him in, Hedge," the duchess told him.

Fear blossomed within her. "Kilby, I do not know
if I can face Rowan," Maura said, throwing aside the
blanket and smoothing out her dress. "If he has come
to chastise me for Everod, I—"

Kilby clasped both her hands and squeezed them in
reassurance. "You have to face Mr. Lidsaw eventually,
and I think it best that it be done in front of friends,"
she said, attempting to soothe Maura's nerves. "If the

gentleman is as ruthless as his elder brother, then Hedge will oblige us, and cast the uncouth scoundrel out on his backside."

"Maura," Rowan said, his voice filled with relief and tenderness as his gaze settled on her.

Her own relief was so great that Maura's knees gave out, and she sank promptly back onto the sofa.

W ell, well, what do we have here?"

Everod peeled his lips off Marjorie's at the sound of Ramscar's voice. He glanced up to see Brawley, Solitea, Cadd, and Ramscar glowering at him. "Good evening, gents. May I introduce you to Marjorie."

"G'evening, sirs," the barmaid said, her eyes widening at the four handsome strangers. The greedy wench was likely tallying the riches she could earn if all five of them would buy her favors for the evening.

Cadd snorted. "So typical of you, Everod. We've been racing all over town, worried we'd find you battered, bloody, and with someone's broken teeth buried in your fist. And here you are cuddling up to some whore."

"Say, I have ears, you know!" Marjorie exclaimed.

"There is blood on his mouth," Brawley dryly observed.

Snickering, Solitea swore and retrieved his handkerchief. He tossed it at Everod, who deftly caught it. "Rouge, I think. The color looks lovely on you, Everod."

He must look like a bloody idiot with lip paint smeared on his lips. Everod nudged the barmaid off him, and used Solitea's handkerchief to wipe away the evidence of her kiss.

"Marjorie, my sweet," Everod said without looking at her. "Since I was about to decline your generous offer before we were rudely interrupted, why don't you fetch some beer for my friends."

Vexed that his friends had deprived her of some extra coin, the barmaid stomped off to the bar. Everod dropped the soiled handkerchief on the table and silently watched as his friends sat down at his table.

"You seem to have recovered from losing Miss Keighly rather swiftly," Solitea observed casually as he glanced at the buxom barmaid. "So this evening's debacle was more about striking at your family, rather than anger over the fact the lady was planning to marry your brother."

Everod's shoulders tensed. Another night he might have launched himself at his friend, and physically displayed his displeasure, but he was not the only man at the table poised for an attack. The four of them were battle-ready. They expected him to be unreasonable, perhaps even violent. Just to prove he wasn't a wild animal that they needed to subdue, Everod deliberately leaned back and relaxed.

He cracked his neck, and smiled faintly at his friends. "My feelings are my own business, Solitea. Marjorie was just being friendly. She runs her own business within Xavier's establishment. I was about to refuse—"

"A bit late, don't you think?" Cadd snapped, gesturing at the ruined handkerchief. "Your Marjorie had her hand curled around your stiff cock, and her tongue—"

"She isn't my Marjorie, you arse!" Everod growled over the marquess's diatribe. "I barely know the wench. Besides, even if I was going to fuck her, it would have been my choice, *my* business!"

"Everod is correct," Brawley said, placing a placating hand on Cadd's arm. "It is none of our business, and we will be happy to leave, so you can continue your conversation with the lady."

Marjorie returned with their beer, and took her time placing a pot in front of each gentleman. Her gaze roamed possessively over Everod, sending him a silent invitation that was difficult for the other men to ignore.

"If you feel inclined, my lord, you may say your farewells to me in private." The barmaid winked at him. "You know where to find me."

Cadd slammed his fist on the wooden table. "By God, you have gone too far, even for you!"

It appeared that little provocation would prod the marquess to violence this evening. Since the four men had hunted him down to save him from his temper, the irony was not lost on Everod. "You have something to say, Cadd?"

"Yes. If you want to know the truth, I feel *inclined* to smash your face in," Cadd said, bracing his palms on the table as he pushed himself onto his feet.

Everod slowly stood. "You could try."

Both Solitea and Ramscar jumped up and seized Cadd's arms to prevent him from attacking.

"This isn't helping," Solitea murmured in Cadd's ear.

The marquess scowled at Everod as he strained

against his human shackles. To Solitea, he said, "Miss Keighly is at your house miserable because of this bastard, while he celebrates her ruination with some tavern whore. I agree with your duchess. We are on the wrong side of this business."

The urge to fight Cadd drained away at the mention of Maura's name. He grabbed Solitea's arm. "Maura is at your house."

Solitea hesitated, seeming reluctant to confirm her whereabouts. "Yes. Kilby, my sister, and Patience thought it best that Miss Keighly return to our house instead of the Worringtons'."

After you humiliated her, where was she supposed to go?

In the ballroom, Everod had been completely caught up in his own roiling emotions. His feelings of betrayal because Maura thought that she could marry Rowan, his jealousy at his brother for being in the position to claim her, and his hatred for his father's countess had blinded him. He had attacked without thinking of what would happen to her once he spoiled Rowan's plans to marry her.

What did you expect, Everod? That Maura would forgive you for humiliating her in front of half the ton, *and that all would be as before?*

The Worringtons would send Maura away. She would return to her parents, and steps would be taken to insure that he never saw her again. Georgette would be furious that her plans had been ruined. Although Lady Worrington would not have been able to strike at him, Maura would have suffered greatly in her aunt's hands.

You've lost her forever.

He had wondered, in the ballroom, if he had misunderstood Maura's silent message to him when she had begged him not to carry out his revenge on the Worringtons. She had not been trying to protect Rowan or her reputation. Perhaps she had been begging him not to destroy what they had shared together.

She had offered him love, and pride and jealousy had caused him to reject it. He had not believed, or trusted, Maura enough to risk opening himself wholly to her. This evening he had severely punished her for the pieces of himself he had unwillingly surrendered to her, because she had tamed some of the wildness within him.

He had been vulnerable to her.

"Is Maura still at your house? I want to see her," Everod appealed to Solitea, knowing he would fight all of them if they tried to keep him from seeing her.

"No!" Cadd shouted, his look scathing. "We came to prevent him from wiping out his clan or maiming some fool who wandered into him."

"The night is early, Cadd," Everod said, moving so their faces were inches apart. "One less fool in the world won't trouble my sleep."

Brawley stood. He seemed unaware of the tension around him. "It might not be wise, Everod. Miss Keighly was upset and the ladies—"

"There was talk of gelding you," Ramscar added a little too cheerfully.

Everod visibly cringed. The thought of Maura wielding a knife was truly terrifying. "I have to see her tonight. The Worringtons and her family will never let me near her. I may never get another chance."

A chance for what? To beg for her forgiveness? A chance to say farewell? A prideful man, Everod found neither option palatable, but he owed Maura something more than his cruelty.

Solitea must have pitied him when he noted the confusion and vulnerability he saw on Everod's tortured visage. His friend had guessed he was in love with Maura Keighly before he had. Mayhap it was because the man had suffered his own trials with his duchess.

"We'll take you to her," Solitea said solemnly.

Realizing belatedly that there were three other ladies present, Rowan Lidsaw retreated behind a formal demeanor. He crossed the room to Kilby, and bowed. "Forgive my intrusion, Your Grace. It has been a difficult night for my family." He shot a quick glance at Maura. "My cousin's whereabouts were not known to us until I revisited the Kerstings, and learned a negligent footman had not delivered your message to my family."

"Oh, you poor man," Kilby said, taking him by the elbow and leading him into the drawing room. "Lord and Lady Worrington must have been overwrought. In our defense, we thought it best for our dear friend to depart the ball before Lord Everod decided to further abuse Maura's good name."

Rowan visibly relaxed at the duchess's censorious tone when she spoke of the viscount. It had been brave of him to approach the household of one of his elder brother's closest friends. He risked facing not only Everod, but *les sauvages nobles* en masse. From Rowan's narrow perspective, the Soliteas' town house was a veritable lion's den.

"You are kind to welcome me into your house, Your Grace," Rowan said, kissing the duchess's hand. "My family is indebted to you and your friends for protecting my cousin from the cruelty of the *ton*."

"Have you met my dear friends?" Kilby swiftly introduced Everod's brother to Fayre and Patience.

"It is a pleasure, ladies," Rowan said, his enthusiasm fading into regret. He turned to face Maura. "With your permission, Your Grace, I would like to speak with my cousin."

"I would not presume to stand in your way, Mr. Lidsaw," Kilby said, charmed by the young gentleman's impeccable manners. "However, you should be aware that I have invited Maura to stay with us. If she agrees, then you will be returning to the Worringtons without her."

"I can understand your reluctance to speak with anyone bearing the Lidsaw name, Cousin," Rowan said, crouching down so he was eye level with Maura. "However, I have not come to judge you."

"Come, ladies," Kilby said, gesturing to her friends. "Maura and Mr. Lidsaw desire some privacy."

Maura bit her lower lip to keep from laughing as she watched the trio move to the opposite side of the room. A blue Chinese vase in the corner seemed of some interest to the ladies. Maura was moved by their silent support. "You did not have to come for me, Rowan. I would have eventually returned home."

"I would have come for you sooner." He took her hand. "Initially, no one knew where to find you. Georgette thought you were hiding somewhere in the Kerstings' house. A search commenced. Then Father began to weaken, and I thought it best to send them home. Besides, I wanted the opportunity to speak with you alone."

He nodded at the ladies, who were pretending not to eavesdrop on the couple's conversation. He smiled at Maura, amused at the duchess's broad interpretation of the word *privacy*.

"What is there to be said?" Maura softly asked. "Your brother—"

Rowan scowled. "Everod has made things damn awkward between us. If you think I blame you for his callous actions, I do not," he said, rushing his words as if he feared Maura would not allow him to finish his speech. "Georgette should have prepared you. My brother has a rather notorious reputation and has never lacked for lovers. He probably recalled your youthful affection for him, and sought to exploit your sweetness, your generous nature. What you did not understand was the resentment he holds against our family. Everod's heart is ice. Revenge was his goal, when he whispered loving words in your ear."

Rowan was the last person with whom Maura intended to discuss the details of Everod's seduction. How could she explain that his brother had not seduced her with false promises? She had been drawn to Everod in an elemental way beyond her comprehension.

His soul simply called to hers. Or so it had seemed.

Everod had seemed to forget his quest for revenge against his family when he was with her. She had made him laugh, and there was compassion within him, though he loathed acknowledging it. Maura blamed herself for idealizing his carnal need for her. Everod might have lusted for her body, enjoyed her company, but his affection for her had not extended beyond sating his physical needs.

Maura stared at his gloved hand. "Though it might soothe my pride to charge your brother with villainy, I must confess that I went to him willingly. He used no lies to sway me."

He was taken aback by her quiet admission. "Oh. I see." Rowan visibly struggled to digest her words. "Do you love my brother?"

A single tear leaked from the corner of her right eye, and rolled down her cheek. Maura blinked rapidly to banish the rest that threatened to fall. "My feelings for Everod are complicated," she hedged. "And I fear my reply will cause you to pity me."

"Never," Rowan said, using his thumb to wipe away the evidence of her tear. "Instead, I pity my brother for not appreciating the gift you had offered him."

Her heart.

Straightening, Rowan did not release her hand. "I want you to come home with me."

Maura mournfully shook her head in denial. "I cannot face your father and Aunt Georgette. Not yet. I have ruined everything."

"No you haven't," he said, tugging on her hand, urging her to stand. "What Everod said this evening, what he did—it does not matter to me."

One of the ladies gasped in surprise, but the sound had been so faint, Maura did not know its source.

Maura was unconvinced. No man forgave a betrayal so easily. Everod was proof of that. "You cannot mean that, Rowan."

His expression turned indulgent. "Maura, nothing has been ruined. I have already told the family. I still want to marry you," he said, cupping her face. His face was so earnest she could not help but believe he spoke the truth. "I love you, Maura Keighly. Is it possible that you could learn to love me?"

Rowan's understanding was crumbling her hard-won composure.

He immediately sensed her torment. "You do not have to give me an answer. You seemed so confused, and I wanted you to know my feelings. Just come home. My father and Georgette need to see for themselves that you are unharmed by Everod's machinations."

Maura nodded mutely. In spite of Rowan's protests, she felt ashamed of her choices. Rowan Lidsaw was a good man. All along, her aunt had been correct. He would be a kind and decent husband to her.

Then why had she fallen in love with the wrong brother?

CHAPTER 23

"Where is she?" Everod said, bursting into the drawing room unannounced. His four friends entered seconds behind him.

Lady Fayre had been reading a book. She yawned and blinked sleepily at him. "If you are referring to Miss Keighly, she has gone."

"Everod, really," Patience chided as she stood to greet her husband. "You have devastated poor Maura. Do you think a clumsy apology will suffice?"

If he had been capable of it, he would have blushed. Everod had hoped Maura would have been satisfied with his apology.

"Which one of you put Everod up to this?" Kilby demanded, sitting up. She had fallen asleep while the ladies awaited their husbands' return.

"No one. This was Everod's brilliant stratagem," Solitea replied, giving his wife a kiss on the nose. "Nodded off again, eh?"

His wife rubbed her eyes. "It is getting rather embarrassing. Did I miss anything?" she asked her friends.

"Nothing." More alert, Lady Fayre gave Everod a shrewd look. "You might as well take another nap,

Kilby. Lord Everod is not finished, and I doubt our husbands will abandon him."

Something had happened. Lady Fayre was not bothering to disguise her satisfaction or her willingness to toy with him. "What makes you so certain, my lady?"

"Do you think we should tell him?" Patience asked.

"Tell me what?" Everod bit out each word, his frustration increasing with each passing second.

"Mr. Lidsaw came for Maura," Lady Fayre said sweetly.

Ramscar frowned. "Forced?"

His wife replied, "Not at all. Mr. Lidsaw was a gentleman."

Unlike him.

Whether Maura left willingly or was compelled by threats, Everod needed to see her.

Brawley noted Everod's determined expression and cursed. "You think to confront Miss Keighly. At this hour?"

Everod snorted. He did not give a damn about the late hour. He had come to see Maura, and she had escaped him with Rowan's help.

Never again.

"Oh, one more thing," Kilby said, as Everod tried to walk out the door. "Your jealous tantrum at the Kerstings' ball was for naught. Your brother still intends to marry Maura."

Wordlessly, Everod walked out of the room.

Maura entered her aunt and uncle's town house with trepidation in spite of Rowan's assurances to the contrary. She was braced for disappointment and condemnation. What she did not expect was to find her aunt sobbing in the arms of an unknown gentleman.

Aunt Georgette lifted her cheek from the man's shoulder, and stared at Maura and Rowan, her face a mask of absolute misery. It took her aunt a moment to recognize them.

"Oh, Maura!"

Stepping away from her companion, the older woman held open her arms as she strode toward her niece. Casting a worried glance at Rowan, Maura ran to her aunt and the ladies embraced.

"Pray forgive me, Aunt Georgette," Maura murmured into her aunt's hair. "I did not mean to worry you. I was so upset when I left the Kerstings' ballroom. I needed to be alone."

"I understood, Maura," Georgette said, pulling away and holding out her hand to Rowan. "No, my darlings, I have grave news about Worrington." As she squeezed Maura tightly, her aunt's tear-ravaged gaze sought out and held her stepson's. "As you both are aware, the earl has been recovering from an illness. His health was improving. So much so, he had insisted on attending the ball this evening. All of the excitement must have been too much for him. He collapsed in our bedchamber. I immediately summoned Dr. Burke—"

Rowan had heard enough. "Where is he?"

Aunt Georgette blinked. The question seemed to confuse her for a moment. "Upstairs. He is resting."

Rowan released her aunt's hand, and ran up the stairs. Dr. Burke, the gentleman who had been

consoling Georgette when she and Rowan had entered the house, chased after Rowan. The physician
was speaking rapidly, attempting to prepare the
young man for the shock that was to come.

"Surely Worrington's condition will improve,"
Maura said, tilting her face up toward the empty upper landing where Rowan had disappeared. A door
opened and closed in the distance.

Georgette covered her trembling lips, and briskly
shook her head. Several minutes passed before she
spoke again. "Dr. Burke thinks Worrington's heart is
failing him. Illness and old age are the likely culprits.
Regardless of the cause, I am about to lose my husband, and I cannot bear it!"

Her humiliation this evening seemed trivial in
comparison. Maura closed her eyes, thinking only of
her uncle who lay dying upstairs. "What can I do?
Should I get you something to eat, or tea?"

Her aunt rewarded Maura for her thoughtfulness
by pressing a kiss on her cheek. "Nothing for me, my
treasure. Worrington will want to see you. Earlier, he
was asking for you and Rowan."

What about Everod?

It was on the tip of her tongue to ask, but her uncle's grave condition would not benefit from another
upset. Clinging to each other, the pair climbed the
stairs, not speaking until they reached the earl's bedchamber.

Dr. Burke stood outside the room, giving Rowan a
private moment with his father. "Lady Worrington, I
must insist that your visits with the earl remain brief.

Say or do nothing to upset him. If we are to see him through this, he must rest."

"Of course, Dr. Burke," Georgette said, bringing her handkerchief up to the corner of her right eye.

He gave her a fatherly smile. "I left some medicine on the table. Six hours hence, you may add a few drops of the tincture in some warmed wine. It will ease his discomfort."

Georgette touched the physician's hand. "Thank you. You have taken such good care of my husband."

Dr. Burke patted her aunt's hand. "Have someone summon me, if I can be of further service to you."

Maura walked into the earl's bedchamber while Georgette said farewell to the physician. Rowan had placed a chair beside his father's bed. His head bowed, he held the earl's hand.

Maura was startled by the transformation in the earl's appearance. Gone was the rosy vitality and humor that she had witnessed earlier when they had traveled by coach to the ball. Worrington's face looked ashen against the pillows, his mouth narrowed into a pained grimace. His free hand was curled like a claw as he reached for her.

"Maura," he said, panting as if he could not draw in enough air to sate his lungs.

She rushed to his bed. "Uncle." She clasped his hand, silently willing him to get better. "What happened? Are you in much pain?"

"A little," the earl lied, and Maura kissed his hand. "I terrified your aunt when I collapsed. I think I hit my head."

Worrington gritted his teeth as his entire body tightened as the pain tormenting him increased.

Concerned, Maura looked at Rowan. "You should not attempt to speak. Dr. Burke insists that you rest."

"I will," Worrington promised, settling back onto the mattress when the pain ebbed to tolerable levels. "Rowan. Maura. I have little time left."

Rowan stirred in his chair. "No—"

"I'm dying," the earl stated bluntly. "Burke tells me that my heart is worn out, and I trust the man to know his business."

Tears clung to Maura's lashes, blinding her. "You are stubborn, Uncle. You might prove Dr. Burke wrong."

"I need to get my affairs in order. Georgette will summon my solicitor to the house in the morning." Worrington released her and Rowan's hands. Curling his body away from her, he coughed violently into his hands.

Maura went to the small side table near the bed. On the surface were several small dark-colored glass bottles, a glass, and a pitcher filled with water. She filled the glass and brought it to him.

"Should I see if Dr. Burke has left the house?" she asked.

Georgette entered the room. "He has already departed." Worried, she approached the bed. "What has happened?"

"Nothing, Wife. I am fine," Worrington said, pushing the glass of water away after a few sips. "I was about to tell Rowan and Maura about what we discussed earlier."

"What do you need, Father?" Rowan said, using his handkerchief to blot the sweat on the earl's forehead and temples.

"Assurance," Worrington whispered. "Rowan, I need you to promise me that your brother's unfounded accusations toward Maura have not ruined your plans to marry her." He gazed at his countess. "I want you and Maura settled."

"Your concern is unnecessary, Father," Rowan said, seizing Maura's hand and pulling her to his side. "Maura has agreed to marry me."

"Rowan!"

She had done no such thing. In the coach, Rowan had pledged his commitment to her, but she had not offered her consent. Her reluctance had hurt him, but he had agreed to give her more time.

"Now." Worrington shuddered, struggling through another bout of pain. "If you leave now, you can be married in a few days. In Scotland."

Run away to Gretna Green? Maura fought down the surge of panic that originated in her stomach. What little control she had on her destiny was just plucked from her hands.

"I cannot marry without my parents." She stared helplessly at Rowan, begging him to understand.

Georgette placed her arm around her. "Your parents will understand. They have watched you and Rowan dance around each other for years. In my last letter to my sister, I alerted her that we would likely have some good tidings on their return from India."

"My dying wish, Maura," the earl said, swallowing thickly. "I have always thought of you as a daughter.

Honor me, and make the truth. Return to my bedside as my son's wife."

Rowan's grip crushed her fingers. It was a silent warning not to upset his father by denying his last wishes. Maura took a deep breath and nodded. "I will marry your son."

CHAPTER 24

Everod was the first to climb out of the coach. His brisk stride took him up the steps to the front door of his father's town house. The closed door meant nothing to him. He had scaled the garden walls on several occasions for a chance to speak with Maura. Only hours earlier, he had entered the house, and walked the corridors as if he had the right to do so.

He was Worrington's heir, and Maura seemed to be the only person in the family who cared to remember that fact. She had loved him for years. He had despised her just as long. When he had approached her at the bookseller's, she had been terrified that he intended to hurt her. Nevertheless, she had forced herself to see beyond his resentment and tried to touch the boy she had loved. His motives had not always been so noble when it came to Maura, and yet, she had gifted him with her innocence.

It was the only thing she had to sacrifice that would truly cost her. She had gambled recklessly, trusting a man who had once planned to take her virginity and mockingly toss her gesture at her feet.

And how had he repaid that trust? He had allowed

his anger and jealousy of Rowan to provoke him into publicly shaming the one woman who had loved him unconditionally, scars and all.

Maura loved him.

The realization seeped deep into his bones, warming parts of him that he never comprehended were cold. Maura had always loved him, but she had never given him the words.

Even if she had, Everod would not have believed her.

Lovers had whispered of their love into his ear, and he had given the words back to those now faceless specters, because the three simple words would have given him what he wanted.

The one woman who deserved those heartfelt words had never heard them from his lips.

Would she have believed me, if I had had the courage to utter them?

Everod sensed his friends coming up from behind.

"Are you going to knock?" Solitea asked.

Like the other men, he was tired and longed for his wife and his bed.

Everod scowled at the door.

His brother planned to marry Maura.

Not bloody likely.

Everod lashed out with his foot, and kicked in the door.

"Christ, Everod! I said 'Knock'!" Solitea shouted at him as Everod used his body to complete the damage he had done to the door.

He shoved open the door.

Abbot, the Worringtons' elderly butler, had heard the commotion at the door. The man clutched a walking stick in his hands like a cudgel. "Leave this house at once! We don't want your sort here!"

Everod snatched the walking stick out of the servant's hand and tossed it to Cadd. "We are not housebreakers, Abbot. Put on your spectacles. I am Worrington's heir, Everod." He looked past the butler to see if Maura was watching him from behind one of the doors. "I've come for Miss Keighly."

Confusion furrowed the man's brow. He stared at the five intimidating gentlemen, uncertain how he should proceed. "Miss Keighly? I—"

"Who is it, Abbot?" Georgette's crisp tones from overhead had Everod backing up so he could see the countess's face.

With one hand gracefully poised on the railing, she stared down at them all with condescension. "No one summoned you, Everod. This is still Worrington's house. Begone, or I will have Abbot summon the watch."

The butler hobbled forward. "It must have been Dr. Burke, my lady. The heir is usually sent for during these grave circumstances."

Ramscar stepped in front of Everod before he could seize the butler by his nightshirt. "What circumstances, Abbot?" the earl inquired calmly.

"Say nothing," Georgette hissed at her servant.

Abbot shook his head sadly. "Lord Worrington is dying, my lords. Dr. Burke tells us his heart—"

Everod had heard enough. He bounded up the stairs, willing to fight anyone who tried to prevent him from seeing his father.

His father was dying.

Their differences and animosity aside, Everod had never stopped loving his father. The lady who had guaranteed that Worrington had not returned the sentiment stepped in front of him like an avenging angel.

"Worrington does not want to see you," she said, her words cutting him to the quick.

"Well, I love disappointing him," Everod said, brushing by her. He heard his friends talking as they climbed the stairs. Likely, Abbot was giving them more details about his father's ill health.

"No!"

Georgette's shriek made his ears ring. Ignoring her repeated demands that he stop, Everod opened his father's bedchamber door. He paused at the entrance, bringing his fist to his nose. Brightened only by a wall sconce, the interior smelled of vomit, unwashed flesh, and proof spirits.

Everod found his father on the bed. Something was very wrong. Worrington was awake, but he did not acknowledge his son's presence. As he stared straight ahead, his pupils shone like flat glass buttons. The earl's mouth was slack, and his breathing very labored.

"Father," he said quietly, touching his shoulder.

Worrington squinted, trying to focus on his son's face. Everod did not see recognition in the man's gaze, nor did his rambling response make any sense. Half of what the earl uttered was not even words.

"I will get this Dr. Burke," Brawley said, disappearing through the doorway.

Everod pressed his fingers to his eyelids. His father's condition was worsening right before his eyes.

Allowing his hand to slide over his mouth, Everod's

cold forbidding gaze shifted from his incoherent father to the small side table near the bed. It was a dismal arrangement of used drinking glasses and medicinal aids for the sick. He picked up the glass and sniffed the clear contents.

Water.

The small colored glass bottles beside the pitcher of water were not so unassuming. He picked up the dark green bottle and uncorked it. He inhaled, and then winced. The liquid had a sickly foul scent. Everod corked the bottle, returned it to its place, and selected the other bottle. The brown bottle smelled little better, but he recognized it as laudanum. A half-empty glass of red wine was poised at the edge. Everod grasped the glass by its stem and sniffed. The wine had been adulterated with the contents from the dark green bottle.

He careful set the glass back down. His finger touched the cork of the dark green bottle.

"I'm sorry, my friend," Solitea said somberly. There was a gleam of unshed tears in the man's eyes as he watched Everod. He was probably thinking of his own father. The old duke had died suddenly, depriving the Carlisle family of a death bed farewell.

"Can you not let Worrington die in peace?" Georgette whined at all of them. They had invaded her husband's private rooms, and she did not want any of them there.

Maura was missing, too.

She loved his father as her own. If he was dying, she would be at his side, holding her uncle's frail hand.

"Where is Maura?"

The countess yawned delicately into her hand. "Sleeping. If you recall, she experienced a rather traumatic evening because of you."

What had he truly stumbled upon?

Everod curled his hand around the dark green bottle. Angrily, he stalked toward Georgette, his hand closing around her throat as he had done when she had slipped into his bedchamber unannounced.

"You have been busy, have you not, Lady Worrington?" Everod said, his voice pure menace.

"Are you mad? Release me!" Georgette struck his arm with her fists.

Cadd clamped his hand on Everod's shoulder. "This isn't helping."

He glared at the marquess. "She has done something, likely poisoned my father, Cadd." Everod brought his face close to hers. "Maura told me that you have been happily dosing everyone in the household with your teas and tinctures." He recalled seeing one of those ominous colored glass bottles on the tray in Maura's bedchamber.

"The welfare of the staff has always been my primary concern," the countess said defiantly. "I have been gathering herbs for years. No one has perished from one of my remedies."

"Brawley will bring Dr. Burke, Everod," Ram said to his right. "He will verify the contents of all the bottles."

Worrington screamed and thrashed against the mattress. Solitea went to him, attempting to soothe Everod's dying father.

Everod's fingers tightened around Georgette's

throat. "There is no time, and for all we know, Lady Worrington bought his cooperation."

"Y-Your Grace, can you not see that my stepson is as ill as his father," the countess pleaded to Solitea. "I have done nothing wrong."

Everod grinned evilly. "Prove it. I propose a test." He held up the dark green bottle. With his thumbnail, he removed the cork stopper. "If you have faith in your herbal remedies, than I insist that you drink it."

Georgette eyed the bottle warily. "It is very potent." Her throat muscles shifted against his hand as she swallowed. "I usually mix it with wine."

"A few drops, then," Everod said, bringing the bottle to her lips. "At worst, your stewed weeds will sour your stomach."

She turned her face away from the bottle. "No!"

"A few drops or the entire bottle, Georgette," Everod warned. "I do not care. You will imbibe your foul concoction."

He pushed the lip of the bottle against her pressed lips. Ignoring his friends' protests, he added more strength to his constrictive hold. Everod had no compunction about throttling Georgette.

Someone should have done it years ago. The lady was going to swallow some of the contents, even if he had to wait for her to lose consciousness.

"Wait! No!" She kicked and flailed as if Everod held her life in his hands. Her glare was venomous when she met his uncompromising stare. "I will likely die if I drink from that bottle."

Everyone except his father froze at her hoarse confession.

"What is it?" Everod said through clenched teeth. He held up the bottle as if to warn her that her confession might not prevent him from forcing the contents down her throat. "The truth!"

"Several herbs. One of my own special creations. In small, controlled doses, it helps with heart complaints," she said, her eyes cast down to conceal her defiance as she tugged at his fingers clamped around her throat. "Your father has been ill for years, Everod. There is nothing criminal about a wife looking after her husband."

There was no doubt in Everod's mind that his stepmother was lying. If his father had been indeed suffering ill health for years, his informants would have reported it long ago. Maura, certainly, would have told him. In spite of her wariness of his motives, she was too compassionate to keep such dreadful news from him.

"And when someone is careless?" he prompted.

Georgette raised her gaze; her brilliant blue eyes glittered with unshed tears. "Most certainly—death."

Everod could not recall his anguished roar as he shoved the bottle between her parted lips. It took Cadd, Solitea, and Ram to drag him away from Georgette. One moment he was throttling her. Next, he was sitting in a chair across the room with Cadd and Ramscar holding him down by the shoulders. Georgette had fallen to her knees. Everod watched her sob and choke as she stuck her fingers into her mouth. Hunched over, the countess vomited on the floor.

So he had managed to pour some of the liquid down her throat, after all, he thought dispassionately.

Ramscar squeezed Everod's shoulder. "I will summon the watch." The earl strode out of the room.

"Cadd, I am worried about Maura. Find her. Wake her if you must, but return with her," he ordered the marquess.

When his friend departed, Everod crossed the room to Georgette and crouched down in front of her. She had managed to rid her stomach of the poison. Wearily, she sat down on the floor.

"Why?"

His father loved her. Twelve years ago, the earl had banished his heir for her sake. If he had not believed his countess's lies, Worrington would have been forced to accept that he had married a faithless whore.

Visibly shaken by Everod's attack, Georgette gave up her pretense of innocence. "Worrington is thirty years older than I am," she said sullenly. "By rights, I should have been a rich widow."

Her bitter gaze drifted to her husband. The earl's eyes were shut, and the laborious rise and fall of his chest indicated that he still lived. "Healthy old goat," she muttered, pulling her knees up to her chest. "He wasn't supposed to suffer. Lord Perton . . ."

Lord Perton had perished by his young wife's hand as well.

Everod clasped his hands together. "Twelve years is a long time to be married to a man you eventually plan to murder. Why did you wait?"

Her expression grew belligerent. "I do not expect you to believe me, Everod, but I love my husband. He treated me so unlike my other lovers. So tenderly. Anything I desired was mine. I only had to ask."

"Love. Kindness. Respect. Most wives don't become murderous when their husbands treat them well," Everod said, not keeping the sarcasm out of his tone.

"Hypocrite. We are more alike than you will ever admit to yourself or your arrogant friends," she said, leaning forward. She lowered her voice so the others could not hear her. "You were a fool not to accept my offer of a truce. Once your father died, and the title passed to you, I might not have been able to marry you by law, but I would have been your countess," she purred.

Like a spider, Georgette had been weaving her web for so long, she had assumed everyone would blindly follow her. How disappointing it must have been for her when her husband did not die, Maura fell in love with him instead of Rowan, and Everod had not willingly returned to her bed.

Disgusted, Everod stood. He exchanged looks with Solitea. "You will hang for what you have done, Georgette."

She smiled up at him. "I may surprise you. If Worrington lives, he will stand beside me. I will tell him that I had been so concerned about him, that I had carelessly given him too much. Your father loves me," she said, pounding her bosom with her fist. "He will believe it was an accident."

If his father lived.

"There are witnesses who will testify against you."

"You are *nothing* to Worrington," she said spitefully. "You and your friends can challenge me, but in the end, *my* family will support me."

Everod cocked his head curiously at her. Georgette was not behaving like a woman who had gambled for her freedom and had lost everything. She was too confident, as if she had done something clever and he had not guessed her secret.

Cadd rushed into the room.

"Where is Maura?"

The marquess held up his hand to silence him. "I checked all the bedchambers. She wasn't in any of them. So I spoke with the butler." Cadd grasped Everod's arm and shook him. "Rowan was here, earlier. Maura left with him."

Everod whirled around, his amber-green eyes narrowing on his stepmother. "Where are they?"

The room filled with the countess's laughter. "You thought you could take Maura from me." She pushed herself up, staggering slightly as she used the wall to brace herself. "Well, you are too late. Rowan and Maura will be married before you find her," she goaded.

Georgette only laughed at him, when Everod picked her up and shoved her against the wall. "Where did Rowan take her?"

"Across the border," she spat in his face. Her eyes flashing with an unspoken challenge, she managed to look haughty and triumphant as he pinned her against the wall. "Oh, dear, now this is a quandary. Worrington is on his deathbed, and Maura has run off to marry your brother. What will you do? Dash off to rescue your lover?" Georgette shook her head. "A very heroic notion. However, if you abandon your gravely ill father, the magistrate might be swayed into believing that you seduced me, and together we poisoned your father. You have much to gain with his death, and considering our unsavory past—" Her abbreviated shrug quickly turned into a pain-ridden gasp.

Solitea's hand griped Everod's shoulder. "Don't. If she taunts you into killing her, she will have won." When Everod did not respond, he said, "Think of Maura and your father. They need you."

Everod nodded at his friend. As tempting as it was, Georgette would not die by his hand. Somewhere, Maura was alone with Rowan. Bile burned his throat at the thought that he was partly responsible for her being there. "Where are they crossing the border?"

Georgette sneered at him. "If you have a fast horse and the devil's own luck, you might arrive in time to kiss your new sister-in-law."

CHAPTER 25

We are about to be married, Maura," Rowan said indulgently, when she froze at the threshold of the room he had just procured for them at the inn. "No one will think it untoward if we share a bed. Besides, this was the only room the innkeeper had available."

They had been on their journey to Gretna Green for more than a day, and both of them were weary of being jostled within the confines of their coach. When Rowan had suggested that they rest for a few hours, Maura had readily agreed. She had prayed a hot meal and a little sleep would vanquish her increasing melancholy and growing doubts about their elopement.

The meal had consisted of boiled mutton, veal pie, peas and onions, watery potatoes, and a very bitter ale. While the bland food did not satisfy her palate, the hot meal and ale had filled and warmed her empty stomach.

Her brow furrowed as her gaze lingered on the narrow bed Rowan expected her to share with him. Maura doubted she would find the bed as satisfying as their dinner.

Rowan's exasperation flared at her continued hesitation. On a muffled oath, he marched toward her and dragged her into the room. Maura moved to the small hearth, deliberately ignoring Rowan as he exhaled noisily. He was annoyed with her, but she was too numb to care.

The increasing miles distancing her from London had done little to ease the sorrow in her heart. A spiteful part of her blamed Everod for Worrington's failing health. She wondered if he would rejoice when news of his father's demise reached his ears.

"Rowan, do you think he still lives?" she asked, fiercely concentrating on the glowing embers in the hearth.

"Who? Oh, Father," Rowan said, peeling the sleeve of his rumpled frock coat from his arm. He gave the garment several firm shakes before placing it over the back of a chair. "You saw his frail state, love. Undoubtedly, his life has met its mortal conclusion."

Her uncle. Dead. With all that had occurred, the thought was almost too much to bear. Maura glanced in his direction when he said nothing more. Rowan was frowning at her again. She suddenly had a vision of the future. It was filled with years of Rowan scowling at her with the same disappointed expression on his face.

"You believe he still lives."

Her delicate brow lifted at his accusation. "Do you not?"

Agitated, Rowan pushed his hair from his face. "Naturally. What a ridiculous question. I am, after all, his most devoted son."

His gaze narrowed as an unpleasant thought darkened his visage. It spurred him to angrily walk toward her and seize her by the wrists. His thumbs rubbed the fragile flesh of her inner wrists. "And what of your devotion, Maura? Is it as fickle as your heart?"

Maura held his hot gaze. "Fickleness implies loss, Rowan. I can assure you, *you* have never had my heart." She tugged free, distancing herself from the man she had promised her dying uncle that she would marry. The hours alone with Rowan had her questioning the wisdom of uttering vows under emotional duress.

Maura paused in front of the empty bed and swallowed thickly. She felt the heat of Rowan's body a second before he settled his hands on her hips. When she attempted to slide away, he dug his fingers ruthlessly into her joints and held her in place.

"True," he said, sighing into her ear as he rested his chin on her shoulder. "I have been denied both your heart and body. Ironic, is it not, when I am the only Lidsaw willing to marry you. And what of my dear older brother? Did Everod cleverly seduce you into surrendering your virginity with pretty flattery, or did he simply hold you down and take your innocence?"

Maura stiffened in Rowan's embrace. Her earlier exhaustion faded as she became fully aware of her perilous predicament. While Everod had preferred seduction, there was something menacing about Rowan's demeanor. He had subtly changed since they had departed from the Worringtons' household. Her instincts screamed that her betrothed was perfectly capable of shoving her onto the bed and

forcing her to acknowledge his claim if she continued to provoke him.

A single tear slid down her right cheek. "Your
brother is a liar and a cold-blooded villain, Rowan. The
details no longer matter." As she swiped at the tear, she
turned slightly in his arms and pasted a half-smile on
her lips. "You are the man I intend to marry."

Are you certain you have not seen this woman?"
Everod demanded as he shoved the miniature of
Maura he had taken from the Worringtons' household under the innkeeper's nose. Fear and exhaustion
had honed his temper to a lethal edge. "Dark brown
hair. Her eyes are the hue of a storm-tossed sea."
Christ! Next he would be spouting flowery prose
about her lips. "She would have been traveling with a
gentleman."

Everod growled and ground his teeth in frustration
at the man who continued to shake his head. He tried
again. "They would have been traveling in haste.
They might have stopped for the night or merely for a
few hours."

Georgette would have urged Rowan to make the
journey with few stops between London and Gretna
Green. The countess had been wary of Everod from
the beginning, and uncertain of his feelings for Maura.
She would have cautioned Rowan to be vigilant.

"Nay, milord. I would have recalled this comely
lass if I had met her," the innkeeper said, his expression laced with regret. "Run off with the wrong gent,
has she? A shame. I wish you luck on your chase."

Everyone within earshot started at the sound of

Everod's fist slamming against the rough surface of the wooden bar. At that moment, he would have gladly welcomed a fight, but he could not afford the delay. He gruffly thanked the innkeeper and departed.

Everod blinked against the brightness of the sun as he entered the yard. His abused body did not relish another day on horseback, but it was the only way he stood a chance of catching up to Rowan's coach. Wearily, he leaned against a fence while he waited for one of the grooms to bring him a horse. As he had hundreds of times before, Everod opened his hand and glanced down at Maura's portrait. With each passing hour, she was slipping through his fingers. The thought of Rowan touching Maura was enough to send Everod into a mindless rage.

He thought back to the night Georgette had laughed in his face and gleefully told him that it was too late to prevent Rowan from marrying Maura. Her laughter had switched to hoarse curses, when the constable had escorted her from the house. As the hours passed by his father's bedside, Everod had suffered the torments of a damned man, torn between his ill father and the woman he loved. Aye, loved. He was not afraid to admit it to himself when he was on the verge of losing her. Solitea and the others had urged him to go. They had promised to look after Worrington. However, Everod had not been able to abandon his father that night. He was certain Maura would have been disappointed in him if he had.

"I will find you," he told her portrait. There were two more inns along the way that Rowan might have stopped at for meals or fresh horses. In spite of the delays, Everod had the advantage of speed and un-compromising determination. Georgette's influence over his family would come to an end, when he found Rowan.

Everod scrubbed his bearded face with one hand as he stuffed the miniature into the inner pocket of his coat. "Rowan hasn't won, Maura. Even if he marries you, I can promise you that your bridal flowers will be used to adorn his grave."

CHAPTER 26

The bride was terrified. The bridegroom was foxed. It was not an auspicious beginning for a marriage. Or a wedding.

While Maura paced in front of the blacksmith's shop, an elderly gentleman by the name of Mr. Joseph Paisley grumpily waited for the couple who had rudely disturbed his sleep to step within the whitewashed walls and allow him to marry them. Mr. Paisley had even roused two of the villagers from their warm beds to act as witnesses.

Slumped against the side of their coach, Rowan peered bleary-eyed at her. "We—you—promised Father that we would be married, Maura," he said, gesturing with a bottle of Mr. Paisley's fine brandy. "Can't s'pect us to return and tell a dying man his last wishes won't be honored."

Maura wrapped the ends of her shawl tightly around her. It was still dark, they had hours yet until the dawn chased the shadows away. She was cold, hungry, and the long hours confined within the stuffy compartment of the coach with Rowan had not convinced her that he would be the exemplary husband that her aunt Georgette claimed he would be.

"We should have stayed, Rowan," Maura said, thinking of how fragile Worrington's hand had felt in her grasp. "If those were your father's last hours, then he deserved to be surrounded by his family."

Aunt Georgette was alone and likely frightened.

"Enough!" he yelled, allowing the bottle to slip carelessly through his fingers. It struck the ground and toppled over. In the dim lamplight, the brandy reminded Maura of blood.

Rowan reached for her hand and missed. He closed one eye, and caught her fingers on the third pass. "We are going in there. We'll pledge our bloody troths to the anvil priest, and we're married. On the journey home we will con-sin . . . no," he said, shaking his head to clear it. "Consummate our blessed union, and God willing, my father will be still warm for you to hold his hand."

Maura deliberately locked her legs, forcing Rowan to stop. "You make it sound so cold."

"I *am* cold, Maura. And tired." He swiped at his hair, and knocked his hat off. Holding on to her for support, Rowan leaned over in an exaggerated manner and retrieved his hat from the ground.

"Rowan."

"No, no, I've got it." He plopped the hat back on his head. "Georgette s-said you'd be a biddable wife. No fuss. We could carry on like always, and you wouldn't know." He brought his finger to his lips.

Oh, really.

Maura jerked her hand from his grasp. "We? You and Aunt Georgette—"

Good grief, was there a Lidsaw male alive that her aunt Georgette had not bedded?

"Going to be Earl of Worrington someday," he mumbled, snatching her hand and dragging her closer to the blacksmith's door. " 'Course Everod will have to die, too." He blinked at her horrified countenance. "His death should please you, considering he announced to all and sundry that you were his biddable whore."

Rowan frowned. "There's that word again. *Biddable*. I just don't see it."

Maura ignored Rowan's drunken ramblings as she sorted through what he had told her. Aunt Georgette was Rowan's lover. He anticipated inheriting the Worrington title, but two gentlemen would have to die before that could happen.

She brought her hands up to her face.

Aunt Georgette, what have you done?

Maura grabbed Rowan by the shoulder and shook him. "We have to return to London."

He pointed at the closed door. "But—"

"Immediately. We can marry another day," she assured him, wondering exactly when her aunt had begun plotting her husband's death. "Rowan, I believe your father may be in trouble."

He took her hand, drawing her closer to the door. "We'll depart after you marry me."

Maura groaned in frustration. The man had pickled his brain with wine and brandy. "Rowan!"

She was unprepared for his slap, or the viciousness of his sudden attack. Maura spun away from him and collapsed on the ground. He charged her, seizing her arms before she could crawl away.

Maura cried out as he hauled her to her feet.

A subtle slyness had crept into Rowan's expression.

Violence aroused him. The proof was stabbing her in her hipbone. "We have come all this way to marry. Your aunt will be displeased if we return unmarried. So will I," he whispered in her ear. "Georgette loves you like a daughter. Defy me again, and you will break your neck in an unfortunate accident. Your aunt is not the only one who can dispatch troublesome family members without remorse."

For the second time that day, Everod kicked in a front door. Five pairs of eyes confronted him as he strode through the door. After three and a half days of reckless riding and very little sleep, Everod had run out of patience. His ruthless amber-green gaze locked onto Maura's face.

Something akin to what he hoped was relief flickered in his lady's eyes. However, he could not contain his temper, when he noticed that Maura clutched a wilted bouquet of wildflowers in one hand, while her other one was firmly clasped within his brother's.

Rowan gawked at his elder brother as if he were an apparition.

Maura took a step toward him, but his damnable brother dragged her back to his side.

Everod glared at the elderly man who must have weighed close to five and twenty stone. "This marriage cannot take place!"

Rowan swayed against Maura. "Ignore him."

"Och, an' who might ye be, sir?" the grumpy gentleman demanded.

Everod looked her straight in the eye. "The sire of the babe she's carrying in her belly!"

His scandalous announcement awoke the two slumbering villagers who had been called upon to be witnesses.

Maura's sea-gray eyes rounded at his outrageous claim. She jerked her hand free from Rowan's. "T-that is not true!" she stuttered.

His younger brother stepped in front of Maura, blocking Everod's way. "See here, no one wants you here. The lady belongs to me, and—"

Everod slammed his fist into Rowan's jaw. There was a satisfying crack of bone, before his brother dropped to the floor in a boneless heap. He did not know if Rowan had been aware of Georgette's schemes. They could sort out who deserved the blame when they returned to London. He stepped over Rowan's unconscious body.

Maura stared at him. "You hit him."

Everod glanced at his younger brother and shrugged indifferently. "He deserved it."

Her eyes narrowed when he smirked. "So do you!" The crazed woman attacked him, striking him repeatedly on the head with her wilted weeds. "Oh, you do not know what I have endured."

Everod shielded his face with his arm as she relentlessly battered him with her bouquet.

"And then you kick in the door and tell everyone that I'm breeding? What is wrong with you Lidsaw men? Was it not enough that you called me a whore in front of half the *ton*?"

"Marry me."

Maura threw her mangled bouquet at his head. He dodged the floral missile, and it landed on Rowan's back.

"I hate you!" she hissed at Everod.

The elderly gentleman squinted at Maura's stomach. "So are ye carrying this mon's wee bairn?"

"No!" she shrieked, the piercing note an uncanny reminder of her ambitious, murderous aunt.

Everod held out his palms in a supplicating position. "Be fair, my love. We both are aware I was a lost man after I tasted the strawberry jam."

The two villagers straightened in their chairs, listening attentively to the angry bride and her second bridegroom for the night.

He grinned at her. "You might call the afternoon a fruitful endeavor."

Everod had pushed her too far. Maura launched herself into his arms. "Ooph! You take too many liberties, Lord Everod! How can you tease me when your brother is a cruel blackguard—" Recalling her fallen bridegroom, Maura scowled at Rowan and kicked him in the ribs.

Their three spectators winced at her display of violence.

Maura shifted her ire back on Everod. "And you, charging in here like some medieval knight, daring to fight anyone who hurts me." She backed away from him, and sniffed. "Well, you hurt me."

"I know," he said, his heart aching when her eyes filled with tears.

"Really hurt me." She sniffed again, and scrubbed

the wetness on her cheeks. "Shall I have Mr. Paisley punch you or you would perhaps like to do the honor yourself?"

If she wanted to kick him, Everod was willing to lie down on the ground and submit to her abuse. Maura hiccupped into her clenched hand. "This has been an awful day. And—and . . . your father is dying," she blurted out, sobbing.

Everod could not take much more of her misery. It shamed him that he was to blame for much of her upset. Ignoring her muffled protest, he hugged her fiercely. "My father isn't dead. I was with him, before I chased after you. He's gravely ill, but there is a chance he will recover now that your aunt is no longer feeding him poisoned wine every few hours."

Maura gasped and pulled back. "How did you know?"

His amber-green gaze narrowed suspiciously on her. "What do you know?"

Maura sneered at Rowan's unconscious body. If Everod had not been holding her, she probably would have kicked his younger brother again. "Only what he told me. You might want to tie him up before he awakens."

Everod rubbed her back. He never doubted Maura's innocence in the sad affair. "We have much to discuss on the journey back to London."

She nodded absently.

"Marry me, my lady," Everod murmured into her hair. "I love you. You know I did not mean half—"

Maura gave him a pointed look.

Everod sighed. "*All* of the things I said when Rowan stood up and announced that you two were to be married. Marry me, and you, Kilby, Patience, and Fayre can sit around and think of fiendish ways to make me suffer for the pain I have caused you."

The softening started in her eyes. "I love you, Townsend. However, marrying you to claim my revenge seems about as ridiculous as—"

"Seducing a delectable virgin for the same reason," he said, quirking his left brow.

"About my aunt . . ."

Everod did not permit her to finish. Georgette was in the hands of the magistrate. The countess would not escape justice this time. Slanting his mouth over hers, he kissed her as if it had been years instead of days since he last saw her.

Mr. Paisley slammed his hammer down on the anvil. "The pledges av been spoken. The marriage blessed." He nodded at the startled couple. "Ye are wed."

The man pointed at his two companions. "Get some rope. Doona tarry. I'm wanting me bed."

Maura looked up at Everod, her sea-gray eyes gleaming with mirth.

"*I love you.*" She mouthed the words as they moved aside so the men could tie Rowan's hands and feet for the journey back to London.

"I love you, Lady Everod," he said aloud, threading his fingers through hers.

Forged in the hellish fires of pain and betrayal, theirs was a love that could never be broken.